THE EXPEDITION

Bea Uusma is a writer, illustrator and doctor. THE EXPEDITION, the result of a fifteen-year labour of love, won the August Prize in 2013 for best non-fiction book. She lives in Stockholm with her family.

THE EXPEDITION

a Love Story | Solving *the* Mystery *of a* Polar Tragedy

BEA UUSMA

Translated by Agnes Broomé

HEAD *of* ZEUS

First published in Sweden in 2013 by Norstedts Forlägsgrupp, AB, Stockholm
as *Expeditionen Min Karlekshistoria*

This edition first published in the UK in 2014 by
Head of Zeus Ltd.

Copyright © Bea Uusma, 2013
Translation Copyright © Agnes Broomé 2014

This translation has been published with the financial support of the
Swedish Arts Council

9 7 5 3 1 2 4 6 8

A CIP catalogue record for this book is available from
the British Library.

ISBN (HB): 9781781859629
ISBN (E): 9781781859612

Designed and typeset by Lindsay Nash

Printed and bound in Germany by GGP Media GmbH, Pössneck

Head of Zeus Ltd
Clerkenwell House
45-47 Clerkenwell Green
London EC1R oHT
www.headofzeus.com

Table of Contents

Everything in this book is true. It all really happened.

Except pages 240-242.

1.
My love story.

I hate being cold. The mere thought of going outside without mittens on a windy day makes me panic. When the temperature drops below freezing I prefer to stay indoors. I used to work as an illustrator. Then I studied to be a doctor. I buy extra warm socks for my children, so they won't be cold either. I spend hours in the bath. I load the dishwasher. I can't be bothered to load the dishwasher. I have a bus pass and a door code and a fixed mortgage rate. I have a day planner and a play list for jogging and every day, for fifteen years, I have ached to go to this one desolate island, a shard of white in the Arctic Ocean. The island is completely uninhabited and buried under a glacier that falls sharply away into the sea, sheer like a cliff face. It's sometimes called the *inaccessible island*, because it's always embedded in pack ice. Three times I've tried to reach it, but every time we've come close we've been forced to turn back or risk our ship getting stuck or being crushed by the immense, mint green ice floes. Nothing grows on this island, but at its southern tip there's a narrow stony beach, free from ice, a tiny spit of land jutting out into the sea. There's nothing on this beach but crushed rock and gravel, a few pieces of driftwood, and it's to this particular beach I want, no, not want, *have to go*.

I have longed for this beach for fifteen years. I have to get there, even though I don't know what I'll do once I'm finally there. Once I'm finally on White Island.

IT WAS SOME LAME PARTY in the early nineties; I had ended up slumped in an armchair. I took a book down from a bookshelf: *Andrée's Story: The Complete Record of His Polar Flight, 1897.* I started reading. Then I got up out of the armchair and went home. I took the book with me. It has been on my bookshelf ever since. For over fifteen years I have been unable to stop thinking about the Andrée expedition: three men from Stockholm, who disappeared on their way to the North Pole in a hydrogen balloon. The remnants of their final camp were found 33 years later, frost-bound on a desolate island in the middle of the Arctic Sea. Three skeletons, a small, tattered tent. The more I learn about their story, the more real it seems, like a black and white photograph gradually filling with colour.

The history of polar exploration is full of heroic expeditions. At the end of the nineteenth century, when the Arctic and Antarctica were still white spots on the world map, there was no shortage of men who would bravely throw themselves into the unknown. Hard men with hoar frost in their beards – Nansen, Amundsen, Nordenskiöld – who after unthinkable trials returned as national heroes. Royal honours. Happy endings. The Andrée expedition was nothing like that. With hindsight it is clear they should never have set out at all.

A few weeks after the party, I was driving from Stockholm to Gothenburg. About halfway there, as I was passing Gränna, I stopped by the Andrée Museum. Something happened to me when I saw the expedition's gear with my own eyes for the first time. I walked from display to display for hours, ogling tin cans scarred by polar bear teeth and sledges with improvised repairs. Back in my car on highway 40 I kept my eyes on the road, but I could not stop thinking about what I had seen. I tried to talk sense into myself, but I was like a vampire tasting human blood for the first time. It became *my* expedition.

I returned to the museum. I began buying books about the Andrée expedition in second-hand book shops. I began searching for something, without really knowing what. The only thing I knew was that I had to get inside the expedition, as deep inside as I possibly could. When there were no more books to read I turned to the original documents from the end of the nineteenth century in the museum's archive: from Andrée's hotel bills and order forms, wills and records of maritime declaration hearings to love letters, each page crammed heartbreakingly full, and private messages on the backs of photographs. I have stared at ugly little school drawings of dogs, without understanding what I was looking for. And still I have kept on searching. The youngest member of the expedition was newly engaged when he disappeared. I have met with his relatives. And hers. I have tracked the lives of the three explorers, gone through parish registers, land registry records and Stockholm's civil census data. I have visited the houses where they lived. Stood in their stairwells.

There is a mystery at the heart of the story of the expedition, which remains unsolved: we don't know why they died. It is like a medical whodunit: at 1.46pm on 11th July 1987 the balloon the Eagle took off from Spitsbergen and disappeared into the clouds, heading north. Four days later one of their homing pigeons returned. A few buoys washed ashore along the coast. Then there was only silence, for 33 years. The bodies of the members of the expedition were found by accident in 1930 on White Island, an uninhabited island in the Arctic. Their diaries, found at the campsite, tell of how they were forced to make an emergency landing, just three days after take-off, setting their leaking balloon down in the middle of the arctic pack ice, and of how they man-hauled their sledges, each weighing many hundreds of pounds, across the ice for three months, perpetually cold and wet, in an attempt to make it back to dry land. Once they reached White Island, after 87 days of inhuman exertion, all entries cease. They had ample provisions, warm clothing, functioning weapons and several crates of ammunition. But the three members of the expedition died, before they had even unloaded their sledges.

The pages of the diaries, frozen solid on White Island, have been successfully preserved, so the text is actually still legible. The rolls of film found in the camp could be developed, even though they had been buried under a blanket of snow for over three decades. But despite the diary entries and the photographs taken while on the ice, no one has been able to solve the mystery of how the members of the Andrée expedition met their end. As soon as they stepped onto dry land on White Island, something happened. Something they did not write about. Ever since 1897, writers, journalists, doctors and polar researchers have tried to determine what really happened. But no one has been able to scientifically prove the cause of their death.

1.   The three members of the Andrée expedition, Salomon August
Andrée, Nils Strindberg and Knut Frænkel, reached White Island on
5th October 1897. For the first time in three months they pitched their
tent on solid ground. The polar night, four months of uninterrupted
darkness, was imminent. They were aware that their chances of being
rescued during the dark season were non-existent. Since no one would
come looking for them at White Island, an uncharted island, they
would have to winter on its shores. Come spring they would be able to
strike out for one of the depots that had been prepared along the north
coast of Spitsbergen, and hope to be found in due course.

2.   It *is* possible to survive a winter on an uninhabited island 870
miles north of the Arctic Circle. Andrée was well aware that two years
previous, the Norwegian arctic explorers Nansen and Johansen had
wintered successfully in a small hollow on Franz Josef Land, at almost
the same latitude as White Island, in the same sector of the Arctic.
(Nansen and Johansen developed bedsores from spending the whole
winter lying side by side in the hollow. But when they managed to make
it back to civilisation, Nansen had put on twenty-two pounds. Johansen
had gained thirteen.)

3.   The group had enough food and water to survive a wintering. Aside
from tinned goods and dried food they had fresh meat from animals
killed along the way (polar bear, bearded seal and birds, particularly
ivory gulls). According to their calculations their meat stores should
have lasted through the polar night. Their Primus stove was designed
for cooking and to melt snow for drinking water when used. When
the camp was discovered in 1930, there was still paraffin in the stove.

Testing revealed that after 33 years on White Island, the stove was still fully functional. There were more than one hundred boxes of matches in the camp.

4. Aside from the clothes they had on, their sledges held plenty of extra clothing to help keep them warm: woollen jumpers, oilskins, fur hats, mittens, socks and boots. They had a tent, two polar bear pelts, several blankets and a reindeer skin sleeping bag.

5. They had medicines, three working rifles and crate upon crate of ammunition.

WHAT HAPPENED NEXT IS UNCLEAR,
BUT WE KNOW THE FOLLOWING:

1. There was a blizzard on 6th October.

2. On 7th October, after two nights on the island, they moved their tent to the lee of a small crag, 900 feet from the water's edge. They started gathering the driftwood scattered across the beach into piles. They planned to build a hut to winter in.

3. The storm forced them to stay in the tent on 8th October. Three days had passed since the expedition made landfall on White Island. At this point Andrée stopped making diary entries.

4. We don't know the timeframe, but something caused the death of the youngest member of the expedition, Nils Strindberg. We know that he was survived by at least one person, because he was buried under rocks in a crevice. But neither Andrée nor Frænkel made any notes about this event.

5. It is not known whether Andrée and Frænkel died at the same time. It is not known whether one of them died and the other remained alone. Neither one was given a grave.

How did they die?
Why did they die?
What really happened?

I WAS IN MY THIRTIES THAT NIGHT when I took the book and left the party, but I first heard about the Andrée expedition as a child. When I was twelve, my sister and I wrote a song for the Eurovision Song Contest.* The song was called *There's trichinosis in it!* The title referred to the polar bear meat Andrée, Strindberg and Frænkel ate to survive on the pack ice. Trichinella is a parasite that infests animals and can be transmitted to humans through consumption of undercooked meat. During the 1970s and 80s the members of the expedition were widely believed to have died of trichinosis. Today we know that trichinella infection is virtually never fatal.

The Andrée expedition is Sweden's most oft-depicted polar expedition. More than 50 books have been written on the subject, almost all of which end the same way: the exhausted group reach White Island. Nils Strindberg dies first, feverish and racked by seizures, his body no longer able to withstand the trichinosis. Salomon August Andrée and Knut Frænkel are also weakened by trichinella infection and pass away side by side in the tent. When I read the books, one after the other, I realise that the authors cite each other in their musings about what might have happened on White Island. Reiterate an assumption often enough and it turns into truth.

* Our song never made it to the Eurovision Song Contest.

WHAT CAN KILL three young people in the course of a few days? Trichinosis is not the only theory that has been put forward. Some have tended toward the scientifically sound, others toward the imaginative. All are based on a very small set of clues.

HYPOTHERMIA, 1930

The Andrée Diaries is the most well-known book written about the expedition. (It was published in 15 languages within three months of the camp being discovered.) It concludes that the members of the expedition must have frozen to death, because their clothes were not suited to arctic conditions.

CARBON MONOXIDE POISONING IN THE TENT, 1931

Cooking inside a snow-covered tent will eventually lead to carbon monoxide poisoning and asphyxiation. Ernst Liljedahl first proposed this theory in his pamphlet *How did the Andrée expedition perish?* Hugo Nikolaus Pallin is in full agreement in his book *The Andrée Mystery* from 1934.

MORPHINE, 1935

Peter Wessel Zapffe was a photographer and part of the group that discovered the camp on White Island. He found a glass vial of morphine at the campsite. Did they kill themselves by taking an overdose? This possibility occurred to Zapffe straight away, but he delayed publishing his hypothesis for five years. He had declined to speak out earlier because the leader of his expedition had told him not to tarnish Andrée's reputation.

TRICHINOSIS, 1952

Doctor Ernst Adam Tryde analysed a small sample of polar bear meat brought back from the campsite and found traces of trichinella cysts. He wrote an entire book about his theory: *The Dead on White Island: The Truth about Andrée.* If you ask people who have heard about the expedition they almost invariably mention trichinosis. But it is, on principle, more or less impossible to die of trichinella infection. Nevertheless, even the website of the Swedish Institute for Communicable Disease Control states that the members of the Andrée expedition are believed to have died of trichinosis.

OXYGEN DEPLETION INSIDE THE TENT, 1953

Arthur Wilhelm Granit has nothing to say about Strindberg's death, but in an article in the newspaper *Hufvudstadsbladet* he suggested that Andrée and Frænkel died of oxygen deprivation in the tent, which the storm had buried under a thick layer of snow.

OPIUM, 1983

No one would willingly spend a winter in a tent on White Island. Glaciologist Valter Schytt has personal experience of wintering in the Arctic and knows the psychological effects it can have. In an article in the medical journal *Läkartidningen* he proposed a theory of suicide by opium overdose.

HYPERVITAMINOSIS A, 1994

Vitamin A is stored in the livers of polar bears and seals and is toxic if ingested in large quantities. The members of the Andrée expedition knew that polar bear liver is poisonous to eat, but they were unaware that the same danger is associated with seal liver. They ate seal liver while on the ice. For some reason this theory never gained much momentum. I have only come across it in a single letter, sent to the Andrée Museum by an American man, R S Woodruff.

LEAD POISONING, 1998

At the end of the nineteenth century, it was common practice to use lead solder to seal tin cans. It has been the cause of death of several wintering polar explorers, who were forced to rely exclusively on tinned goods. The Andrée expedition's stores held a great quantity of tin cans.

The theory was proposed, as one of several possibilities, by Mark Personne, medical consultant and director of the Swedish Poisons Information Centre.

BOTULISM, 2000

Clostridium botulinum toxin type E is one of the world's most potent toxins. It is produced by bacteria native to the arctic seabed and can accumulate in seal meat. The toxin can also be found in canned fish of the type the expedition brought with them. In an article in *Läkartidningen* Mark Personne once again assessed the relative probability of different causes of death. This time he proposed botulism as a possible cause.

....

More than a hundred years have passed. Despite all the theories and suppositions, no one has been able to prove why they died. Having read all the books and seen the same old facts repeated over and over, I realise I have to start fresh, from the very beginning. If I redo the puzzle, from every angle, the shape of the missing piece will emerge, even if it remains missing.

For so many years I have bored uninterested family members, friends and strangers over dinner with details of the worn-down soles of Nils Strindberg's boots. Now I have to finish what has been left unfinished. I have to solve the mystery, but I will never be able to do so without delving deeper into the expedition. I have to walk in their footsteps. I have to reach into their inner pockets. I have to get behind the words on the crumbling pages of their journals. I have to understand what happens to someone stranded on sea ice, with no means of escape. I have to go into the ice, beneath the snow crust. I have to go to the place where they died. I have to go to White Island.

2.
On dry land.

IN THE ARCTIC OCEAN, near the 80th parallel, on an imagined straight line between northern Norway and the North Pole, you'll find Spitsbergen. At the northern extreme of this forbidding archipelago, which is completely barren, is Danes Island. It was the summer of 1897. The thermometer showed minus three degrees, even though it was mid-July. Stockholm lay 1,300 miles to the south. Home was 1,300 miles away.

Everything north of this point is white on the map, marked *Unexplored Region*. It would be another 50 years before the Arctic had been fully explored. Only then did it become clear that there was no land to find, that the whole continent consists of an ice-covered sea; the sectors of the Arctic Ocean were named for the topography of the seabed. Layers of sediment billow thousands of feet beneath the ice, forming the Nansen Basin, the Gakkel Ridge, the Amundsen Basin, the Lomonosov Ridge, the Makarov Basin, the Menedeleev Ridge, the Canada Basin and the Alpha Ridge. Ice, several metres thick all year round, covers the surface of the frigid, salty sea. But no one knew that back then.

At that time, no one had planted his country's flag at the Earth's northernmost point. Explorers had tried to conquer the arctic pack ice in many different ways – on skis, with dog sleds, aboard a big ship frozen fast in drift ice. Salomon August Andrée, director of engineering, managed to secure funding for his idea of elegantly gliding through the air to the North Pole instead, in the most modern vehicle of his day, a hydrogen balloon. To minimise the flight route, he set out from Spitsbergen, the most northerly known landmass on Earth. Sailing before a southerly wind, the little expedition believed they could reach the North Pole in just a few days. They did not intend to land. Instead they would drop a large buoy carrying a written message, as though to mark that *We were here first!* Then their journey would continue to dry land in Alaska, Canada or Siberia, wherever the wind would take them. The expedition consisted of three men from Stockholm, who had spent most of their lives at their desks.

They are in position now. Ready. 1,300 miles from home, on that small speck of rock, off the northern edge of Spitsbergen. Their stores hold Russian roubles, American dollars, starched cravats, white kidskin gloves and pink silk neckerchiefs; Andrée and his assistants must be suitably attired for the triumphant welcome they will receive upon landing.

Salomon August Andrée

Nils Strindberg

Knut Frænkel

SALOMON AUGUST ANDRÉE was 42 years old. He was born in the small town of Gränna and worked as an engineer at the Royal Patent and Registration Office in Stockholm, where he approved or rejected patent applications. He had been to the Arctic once before, but on that trip he rarely strayed out of doors: as the 28-year-old assistant of a research team he spent a month under voluntary house arrest at the Swedish Research Station in Spitsbergen, to test the effects of lack of daylight on facial skin tone. (It was a felicitous arrangement, because the other members of the group had fallen out with Andrée over a miscomputation that caused them to bring an insufficient amount of paraffin, one of the few tasks for which he was responsible.) Andrée's actual dream was to fly a balloon across the Atlantic, but no one would finance that plan. In his capacity as expedition leader he personally handpicked the other members of the group.

KNUT FRÆNKEL, 27, was born in Karlstad and had recently graduated from the Royal Institute of Technology in Stockholm. He claimed to be a civil engineer in his application, but he had had no previous professional experience. Frænkel was to conduct the meteorological observations. He was very displeased with the press photographs taken of him in the run-up to the expedition: *I certainly do not wish to have any of the new profile photographs. I believe the old ones were far superior.*

NILS STRINDBERG, 24, was the youngest member of the expedition. A teaching assistant at the Royal Institute of Technology in Stockholm, he had stellar grades in physics, mathematics and astronomy, and had already been noticed by professors and fellows. He was to photograph the landscape from the air and make position determinations to aid future charting of the polar region. Nils Strindberg was second in command, the one who would lead should Andrée become incapacitated. He had planned to learn some *Eskimo* before departure. But he never found the time.

AN OCTAGONAL BUILDING with flying flags had been erected between rugged peaks and mint green glaciers. The balloon hangar, built on the shores of Danes Island, had detachable board walls that could be dismantled quickly, to allow the custom-made hydrogen balloon inside it to climb skyward when the time for take-off came. The balloon was slumping, half-filled, heavy, on the felt floor. There was not enough gas in it yet to lift it off the ground. An apparatus used for the production of hydrogen gas sat by the water's edge, dragged there across the ice from the expedition vessel. The machine worked day and night, producing gas by dissolving 50,700 pounds of iron filings in liquid sulphuric acid mixed with seawater. The gas was then pumped into the balloon through long hoses snaking their way across the beach, slowly filling the rosy-red balloon envelope.

There was an opening in the middle of the floor of the balloon hangar. Underneath, a hole, three feet deep, had been dug into the permafrost, in which the basket of the polar balloon was going to be placed before take-off. Everything in the stores was meticulously labelled. *Andrée's Pol. Exp. 1896*, was embroidered, in chain stitch, on every last handkerchief and towel, but this was 1897. Every label was one year out of date. They had not managed to leave last year as planned. Propelling the balloon toward the North Pole required a southerly wind. All throughout the previous summer, Andrée had waited for the wind to shift. At the end of August they had been forced to give up and go back home, ahead of the autumn storms.

But this was 1897. A year of anticipation. A new attempt. Nils Strindberg had the night watch. He was sitting inside the balloon hangar, his back against the wall. From in there it almost looked as though the balloon were breathing, swelling and falling languidly. He opened his calendar. On the first page Anna Charlier, his fiancée, had pasted a farewell card. A hand-drawn picture, printed in four colours, of a balloon that has just left the ground. Were he to look really closely he would see that Anna has drawn herself into the picture in pencil, on the ground beneath the balloon. Floor-length skirt, her hair in a bun. Waving her handkerchief.

Seven weeks had passed since they parted. Before embarking on the journey, he had made a will, leaving her everything he owned. Nils Strindberg was 24 years old. He had three months left to live.

It is strange to be sitting here again this year, thinking about how I am engaged to the most wonderful girl on Earth, my dearest Anna. Yes, I may well shed a tear when I think about the happiness I have known, which may never again be mine. But what would it matter if only I knew that <u>she</u> would be happy. But I know she loves me, this makes me proud, and that she would be much moved by my passing. For this reason it must be with melancholy I think of her and the happy times we spent together this winter and, in particular, this spring.

But let me be hopeful. The balloon is varnished and ought to leak much less than last year, summer lies before us with the favourable winds and the sunshine it brings. Why should our endeavour not be successful. I truly do believe in it unreservedly.

ANNA CHARLIER WAS THE YOUNGEST but one of ten siblings, born in the tiny village of Gråmanstorp in the southern county of Skåne. That spring, every weekend had seen Nils Strindberg take the steamer from Stockholm to Johannesdal, the boarding school where Anna worked. She lived at the school and taught the twelve students music. She was a piano teacher and governess.

Anna Albertina Constantia Charlier was 25 years old. She wanted to be a concert pianist.
Her name means hydrogen balloon in French.

IT WAS SNOWING ON DANES ISLAND. The polar balloon floated in its hangar, filled with hydrogen gas, tethered to the ground by hundreds of sandbags. It was snowing, even though Andrée in his speeches in Stockholm had made a point of underscoring the benefits of the constant sunshine and negligible precipitation of the Arctic. The balloon hangar had no roof. It was filling with snow. The ruddy balloon was covered in a white blanket.

The balloon was made by seamstresses in Paris out of triple layers of Chinese silk. It consisted of 3,360 silk squares, each one 12 x 24 inches. It had 8.5 miles' worth of seams. Each seam had been sealed with a silk band. Before the hydrogen gas was switched on, the balloon was filled with air to make it possible to crawl in and seal the seams with varnish from the inside. The basket would be attached to the balloon before take-off. The three members of the expedition would conduct their work on the roof of the basket during their journey to the pole, making meteorological observations, position determinations and photographing the unfamiliar terrain rushing by beneath them.

The basket was not quite large enough to accommodate standing. Nor was it possible for more than one person at a time to stretch out fully on one of the bunks. The basket was connected by a rope ladder to a second story 6.5 feet above the first, a compartment constructed of taut sailcloth. This is where the majority of the stores was packed, in 240 cloth pockets. There were buoys – cork-encased metallic cylinders – in which messages to the outside world were to be placed. The buoys would be dropped from the balloon en route. Thirty-six homing pigeons, a gift from the newspaper *Aftonbladet*, were safely installed in wicker cages. Each cage had food and water bowls, each with a specially designed lip along its edge to minimise spillage during the journey. Capsules for rolled up messages were ready to be tied to the birds' tail feathers. Half of each message was to be composed in normal writing, to *Aftonbladet*. The other half was meant for personal messages and was to be written in stenography. Nils Strindberg had taken an evening course in stenography. He could write 145 words a minute. It was considered very fast. ANDRÉE ANDRÉE ANDRÉE was stamped in capital letters on the underside of each pigeon's wings. Unfortunately there had been no time to train the pigeons to find their way to the newspaper's head office in Stockholm.

The steering mechanism of the balloon, relying on sails and ropes, was a new and modern invention. Long hemp ropes, attached above the basket, trailed along behind the balloon, weighing it down and thus allowing the journey to proceed at an even, constant height. The dragropes consisted of two parts, held together by screw fastenings. Should the longer, lower parts unexpectedly get caught on the smooth ice, they could easily be unscrewed and the journey resumed with only the shorter, upper parts left. Aided by the sails and the friction of the ropes against the ice, the balloon would be *to some extent manoeuvrable* against the wind. That was the idea.

Andrée and the other members of his expedition had spent several years at their desks, focusing on detailed pressure readings, meticulous gas mass measurements, painstaking calculations in notebooks, column upon column. Every pulley, rope and webbing had been costume-made and tested for this journey. Every knot used to tie the ropes had been tested for strength and slippage in pull tests and wear tests. Nils Strindberg had conducted long series of experiments on the performance of the balloon fabric. He had thoroughly examined the density, absorption rate and elasticity of the material in a dedicated machine at the Royal Institute of Technology. He concluded that the selected fabric was completely impermeable. He concluded that the seams between the pieces of fabric were practically as impermeable as the fabric itself.

Knut Frænkel was new to the expedition that year. The year before his position had been filled by meteorologist Nils Ekholm, but as soon as the Andrée expedition returned to Sweden after its summer on Danes Island in 1896, Ekholm had jumped ship. Having seen Andrée's balloon in situ, he had become convinced it would never be able to stay airborne long enough to make it across the North Pole. During the return journey, Ekholm had also discovered that Andrée had refilled the leaking balloon surreptitiously at least seven times, without informing the other members of the expedition.

According to Andrée's initial calculations, the balloon would be able to stay afloat for 900 days. Following a reassessment of his data, he revised that figure down to 30 days. That still meant *fivefold security*: the journey across the Arctic would take six days at most, since they would be travelling at an average speed of 17 miles per hour. No balloon anywhere had, at that time, managed to stay airborne for more than a day.

Originally, the balloon was meant to be called Le Pôle Nord. Changing his mind, however, Andrée christened it the Eagle. It had never been test-flown.

HYDROGEN GAS IS ODOURLESS and colourless. Gas leaking out through the balloon's envelope would have been impossible to detect. As soon as the snow had blown off the top of the balloon, Andrée's crew climbed up. Wearing felt slippers so as not to damage the silk, they crawled around, brushing lead acetate on white strips of fabric which had been laid out along the seams of the envelope, to determine whether there were any leaks. There were. Wherever hydrogen gas was leaking out, a chemical reaction blackened the fabric. They coated the leaking seams with varnish, but there was not enough of it. They had brought too little. Stockholm was 1,300 miles away. Every day they spent on Danes Island, waiting for southerly winds, more and more hydrogen gas was lost. The balloon was refilled. It leaked. It was refilled. It leaked.

Tourist steamers, which had never before braved the inaccessible waters of northern Spitsbergen, had anchored just off Danes Island that summer. Journalists and affluent passengers from all over Europe had come to call, taking turns to traipse around the stony beach in waders. By this time, though, most had given up and gone home.

The members of Andrée's expedition were waiting for the wind to shift.
It was raining and snowing on Danes Island.
The balloon was leaking.
As soon as the wind turned southerly, they would have to set out.

We're travelling aboard a small Russian vessel. The crew is Russian. The food is Russian. I'm the youngest person on board, roughly thirty years younger than the second youngest traveller. When Andrée came here it was called Spitsbergen. Now the archipelago has a new name, Svalbard. It's my first visit to the Arctic. *A journey in Andrée's footsteps*, the advert in the paper had announced. I had no idea there were guided tours to historical polar locations. We're sailing from Longyearbyen, one of the world's northernmost settlements. When Andrée came here there were no signs of human habitation whatsoever, apart from one or two partially collapsed whalers' huts, built of stranded driftwood. The islands of Svalbard consist of jagged peaks, glaciers and moraines. There are no roads. Not a single tree. Almost nothing grows here, just some moss and one or two feeble plants hugging the stones in between the patches of snow, their leaves hardy enough to endure storms and saltwater.

We're going to travel along the coast of Svalbard and see places with a connection to the Andrée expedition: the Swedish research station at Cape Thordsen, inside which Andrée spent a whole winter pouting. Our ship is reinforced to prevent drifting ice floes from tearing the hull open, but it can't break through pack ice. If we're lucky we might be able to strike off across the Arctic Ocean toward White Island, and step onto the beach where the expedition was found in 1930. But only if the waters are ice free. Our ship is no icebreaker.

The other passengers spend their days attempting to take pictures of themselves leaning against the railing while a polar bear walks by in the background. I'm almost disturbingly uninterested in polar bears. I just want to get to White Island.

The first few days on board I'm not cold at all. The cold is peculiar, it doesn't seep into my bones; it just rests against my skin, like gelid quicksilver. We have dropped anchor off Danes Island, where the balloon journey began more than a hundred years ago. The water is so green it looks fake, opaque and almost milky. The polar bear guard disembarks first. As soon as I step ashore I get the feeling something's wrong. Something's off. Then I realise: everything's in colour. I've stared at the black and white photos from the take-off so many times. Now I'm actually here, in the picture. And suddenly everything's in colour.

My boots sink down into the coarse gravel as I walk across the beach. The balloon hangar was torn down long ago. But traces of the expedition are all around me; millions of the iron filings used to make hydrogen gas to fill the balloon cover the stony beach.

The graves of Dutch whalers line the beach. They came to this particular sound in the seventeenth century to catch whales. The ones who died here never got to go home. They were buried in the gravel on this beach, but over the years ground frost has relentlessly broken the handful of planks that cover their bodies, pushing their skeletons out of the frozen soil. I have to mind my step. Andrée, Strindberg and Frænkel must have stumbled over the same femurs and craniums when they were here. I pass the frozen graves slowly. The black eye socket of a skull stares back at me through the gap between two planks.

A few more steps and I'll have reached the place where the balloon hangar once stood. Discarded, fraying rope ends litter the ground. Scraps of fabric, caught in the gravel, flutter in the wind. They must have been part of the felt blanket that covered the floor of the balloon hangar, protecting the envelope from tearing on the rough wood. In the middle of the plateau I can make out a slight depression. It's all that remains of the hole dug for the basket. Andrée, Strindberg and Frænkel stood on this exact spot 37,991 days ago. Focused. Waiting to depart. Now I'm standing here. I'm in exactly the right place, but at completely the wrong time.

Andrée

Strindberg

Frænkel is hidden behind Strindberg

Seconds before take-off

I take back what I said about the cold. It's nothing like gelid quicksilver. Fuck, this place is raw and damp. The wind from the Arctic Sea crawls down my collar and up my sleeves, even though I'm wearing brand new GoreTex polar gear. They wore woollen blazers and knitted mittens.

We never got to White Island, naturally. What was I thinking? It's called *the inaccessible island* because it's always surrounded by pack ice. It's not possible to make landfall on White Island. It's not even possible to get near it.

3.
In the air.

For a brief mom   just now my thoughts flew to you and the loved ones back home. How would our journey turn out? Oh how such thoughts pressed on me but I had to push them aside.

A peculiar feeling, wonderful, indescribable! But we are too busy to get lost in reverie. I take some photographs and then we notice that we are losing height. Ballast is ejected but we dip momentarily. Then we climb again. And now everything seems to be going well. We can still hear chear cheering in the distance.

IT WAS 11TH JULY, 1987. It was a Sunday. Two months previous, Nils Strindberg had cycled up and down the cobbled streets of Stockholm on his new velocipede. He had drunk punsch at Grand Hôtel and shot at pigeons with his air rifle. Now he was standing in a willow basket attached to a hydrogen balloon, half a mile above sea level, leaning against the railing, looking down at ice floes. He was on his way to the North Pole. His feet were cold.

Forty-three days they had waited. Then it had happened. They had been woken up early by the lookout's excited shouts: *Southerly winds! Strong southerly winds!* The flag on the summit behind the balloon hangar had finally changed direction. Like an arrow showing the way, it suddenly pointed unwaveringly north. There was a steady southerly wind, for the first time since the balloon had been ready for take-off.

It was time to go. Andrée, Strindberg and Frænkel: the three members of the expedition supported the decision unanimously. All at once the idling of the past few weeks turned into febrile activity. The crew climbed the wooden scaffolding of the balloon hangar, rushing to dismantle the north wall. Beams and planks broke against the stones of the beach. The 756 pound basket was hauled to the centre of the balloon hangar and attached. Last minute personal belongings were stowed. They hurriedly jotted down a few farewell telegrams, one to King Oscar and one to *Aftonbladet*, handing them to the people remaining behind. Vilhelm Swedenborg, the expeditions alternate, who had travelled with them from Stockholm and who had waited to see if one of the others would pull out so he could take his place, heaved a sigh of disappointment, or maybe it was relief.

Andrée, Strindberg and Frænkel drank a farewell toast of champagne. It was time to go. They climbed into the basket. It was time.

For a few seconds time stopped on Danes Island. The crying seabirds suddenly fell silent. The waves surging against the shore froze even as they crested. Strindberg could not hold back a tear. And then Andrée's voice broke through the silence: Cut everything! But when the hawsers were cut, the balloon failed to take off as planned. Instead it was caught in a heavy squall and thrown into the only remaining wall. The balloon slammed into a corner post before finally climbing skyward. The last thing Andrée was heard saying was, *What the devil was that?*

As soon as the balloon blew free of the wall and soared out across the sound, the wind caught its sails. The balloon started spinning and suddenly plunged toward the sea. Panicking, the members of the expedition began cutting ballast sandbags loose. At the same time, something occurred that no one could have anticipated sitting behind a desk: suddenly the dragropes, which lay stretched out across the beach, all twisted the same way, unscrewing themselves from their fastenings. When the balloon floated out across the water, the ropes had been detached and lay scattered on the beach below. Without dragropes and having ejected over 440 pounds of ballast into the sea, the Eagle was unexpectedly 1,625 pounds lighter and consequently rose rapidly, much too high, straight up into the sky.

The Eagle had lost the lower two thirds of all three dragropes. Without dragropes the balloon's height could not be regulated. And without the friction of the ropes across the ice, the sail would not function. What was supposed to be a well-organised journey to the North Pole and back had instead turned into an uncontrollable aerial voyage, aboard an ungovernable hydrogen balloon drifting before the wind. The crew on the beach expected Andrée to open the vents at any moment, to make an emergency landing on Hollander Head, the small spit of land on the islet across the strait. But he never did. The Eagle disappeared into the clouds to the north.

THREE MEN STOOD ON the roof of the basket, attempting to make new dragropes by splicing together what remained of the old. They were unsuccessful. And yet, the balloon was being carried by the south-easterly winds, straight toward the North Pole.

Half an hour after take-off, Nils Strindberg realised that he had forgotten to drop his farewell letter to Anna. He had put it in a case and made a deal with the crew on Danes Island that they would keep an eye out for when he would throw it overboard, a final gesture. The idea was that he would hit the spit of land across from the beach on Danes Island. The crew would row across and retrieve the case so that it could be delivered to Anna in Stockholm. If everything went perfectly she would have the letter in time for her birthday. That was what they had agreed. But Nils had been too busy. In truth, it had slipped his mind.

Now they were 13 miles away.

At Spitsbergen's northern extreme, on the edge of the Arctic Sea, outermost in the line of islands by Fair Haven Sound, lies Vogelsang. It was not until the balloon drew near the island, which juts steeply out of the frigid, bright green sea, that Nils realised the cliffs, which looked so invitingly smooth from a distance, were actually strewn with large, jagged boulders. He had no choice. It was the last island they would pass before floating out across the pack ice.

He leaned out and flung the case.
He dropped his farewell letter to Anna on an island where no one would ever find it.

THEN THE WIND TURNED. And turned again. Without its dragropes, the rose-coloured aerostat zigzagged above the arctic ice fields. Even though the Eagle was no longer dirigible, drifting in the wind like a toy balloon some child had lost hold of, no one in the little group mentioned their calamity. Nils Strindberg's only diary entry is a stark statement: Guide rope lost. Everything was quiet and still in the basket. Since the balloon was travelling at the same speed as the wind, there was not even a breeze to be felt. The Swedish–Norwegian union flags hung limply. The only sounds were the whistling of the vents and infrequent cooing from the pigeon cages. No one mentioned the reason the vents were whistling: the balloon was leaking. The plan had been to travel across the Arctic Ocean at a constant altitude of about 500 feet. Without the weight of the dragropes the balloon had instead climbed to almost 2,300 feet. At that height the air pressure is so low the hydrogen gas was being squeezed out.

They travelled across an unexplored continent. They journeyed through clouds. No weather forecasts had ever been made for the region north of the 80th parallel, and yet they had been convinced it basked in uninterrupted sunshine. Humidity made the balloon heavy; it had gradually begun losing height. That first evening, at 9.43 p.m., Andrée, Strindberg and Frænkel were forced to drop more ballast – cork buoys and sand. It was not enough. They threw rope ladders and even more sandbags over the side.

During the first night of their journey to the North Pole the wind died completely and the Eagle hung stock-still, shrouded in fog, 130 feet above the ice.

THE NEXT MORNING THE EAGLE'S textile components, ropes, flags, sails and wicker basket had all acquired a glistening white crust. A carapace of ice. Every inch of the balloon was covered in hoar frost. Once again it began to sink, slowly but inexorably. That afternoon, at 3.15 p.m., the Eagle was so heavy with frost and damp it started hitting the ice with regular, heavy thuds. Anything that could be spared was now thrown overboard to help the balloon to rise: sandbags, ropes, a thirty-five pound rope cutter, an iron anchor. At 5 p.m. the three-foot buoy they had intended on dropping at the North Pole, to show that the expedition had reached their destination, was sacrificed. They ejected several hundred pounds of ballast, but to no avail. The balloon hit the ground every two minutes. The thuds were so jarring Nils Strindberg vomited.

They had been sure there would be constant sunshine. They had not reckoned with there being fog and hoar frost in the Arctic. They had also not reckoned with the hydrogen gas slowly seeping out through the eight million microscopic holes made by the sewing machines the Parisian seamstresses used to stitch together the balloon's nine miles' worth of seams.

I visit Svalbard three times. I never reach White Island, because there is too much pack ice in the water. Every trip ends the same way: I try to find out which week of the year is most likely to be successful. Make calls. Check statistics. Puzzle out that it ought to be week 31. Take on extra work. Scrimp. I try to find someone to go with me. Find no one who wants to go with me. I book a place on a chartered boat trip, The Svalbard Tour. The people at the travel agency tell me they can't guarantee we'll reach White Island, which is far from the standard route and which they only visit exceptionally. I take the coach to Arlanda Airport. I fly to northern Norway. I change planes. I fly in over the snow-covered, craggy mountains of Svalbard. I land in Longyearbyen. I catch a bus to the harbour and as I'm standing on the pier about to board they tell me we won't be going to White Island after all, because the ice is impenetrable, the whole way there. Then the boat chugs off along the west coast of Svalbard, which is usually ice free. We see a polar bear up on land. Everyone is happy. Except me.

The third time I unpacked clothes still damp from the arctic air, I figured I needed a new strategy. In my application to the Swedish Polar Research Secretariat I wrote that I was interested in getting as deep into the pack ice as possible, that I wanted to be unable to see land in any direction. Every time they organise an expedition they let a professional within the arts come along for free. I got the grant. The journey, a polar expedition lasting several months, will take me across the Arctic Ocean aboard an icebreaker. On the way back, we'll pass White Island.

The icebreaker crunches its way through the Arctic. It's slow going. Some days we come to a virtual standstill. There are 110 of us on board. We're going to sail across the entire Arctic Sea, 2,300 nautical miles. It never gets dark. No night, only day. The sky is the exact same colour as the ice.

As in 1897, our maps of the Arctic are white. Because there is nothing here. The charts, which are stacked high on the navigation tables in the captain's cabin, are completely empty, page after page of just white. Sporadic numbers here and there, indicating the depth of the ocean, never less than four digits; the sea is always at least several thousand feet deep. We haven't seen the sky once since we left dry land 13 days ago, but tonight a razor thin sliver of bright yellow light cuts through the overcast grey at the horizon. It's strange to think we're on our way to the North Pole when all we do is chug along, straight ahead. There is no sense of going north, toward the top of the globe, at all. We travel along a wide crack in the ice and through the bow facing windows I watch as the wind brushes the top layer of the water, causing the surface to freeze and stiffen. I can see the exact moment it happens.

It's 20 degrees in my cabin. On the other side of the wall, it's minus 20.3 degrees. The wind speed is 34 miles per hour. With a chill factor of 36 below freezing I have to lower my head to my chest whenever I go outside. I have to bend before the wind. I'm not made for this place. No one is. My mobile reception slowly fades as we travel further into the ice, fewer and fewer bars on the screen. Soon I will be gone too.

Wednesday night. No, Thursday. I don't know anymore. I'll never be able to sleep again. It's impossible to feel tired with all this light. We're reversing again. It's twenty to midnight. The icebreaker chomps away, the ice flips over, 10 feet thick and bright turquoise. The world begins and ends with this boat. The world is just the right size. I'm 20 seconds away from a cooked meal on the upper deck, 40 seconds away from my cabin on the lower deck, 15 seconds away from the gym and I make my own schedule, 24 hours a day. A hundred times a day on this boat I catch myself thinking: I'll never forget this. I'll never forget what it's like to bounce around to *The Ketchup Song* in a gym class alongside the bird migration professor, the marine chemist, the buzz cut helicopter pilots, or how we constantly have to parry the lurching motion of the boat. I'm thinking that here we are, bouncing around in the middle of a room, in the middle of an icebreaker taking us across the Nansen Basin through several feet of ice and below our feet the sea is 11,529 feet deep. Were I to fall overboard, it would take me an hour to reach the ocean floor. The water temperature is minus 1.6 degrees.

We are approaching the 80th parallel. Soon we will have gone further north than Andrée ever did.

4.
On the ice.

 H$_2$O(s)

WATER IS A SUBSTANCE with a unique property: it weighs less in its solid form. When water freezes to ice it gets lighter. Ice floats on water. Rather than sink to the bottom, the polar ice floats on the sea. At the point where the Eagle made its emergency landing, the ice sheet was 10 feet thick.

According to Andrée's calculations, the balloon would be able to stay afloat for at least 30 days. The journey came to an end after 65 hours. On the morning of the 14th July, after just three days in the air, Andrée realised they could not possibly go on. The Eagle was completely unable to rise. Yanking a rope to open the balloon's vents, he allowed the hydrogen gas to rush out. Andrée's expedition to reach the North Pole touched down on the 82°56' parallel, 300 miles from its starting point on Danes Island. They made it less than a third of the way to the North Pole. They also failed to set a new latitudinal record. Two years previous, in the summer of 1895, the Norwegian explorers Nansen and Johansen crossed the 86th parallel on skis. The members of the Andrée expedition were well aware of this fact.

The silk balloon slowly deflated and toppled over on the ice. Its stores contained three sledges and a small, disassembled boat. The sledges were intended for the unlikely event of them having to cross solid ground on the very last leg of the journey, to reach the welcoming reception in Alaska, Canada or Russia. The sledges and the boat had consistently been referred to as the emergency gear, additional equipment that until now had attracted no particular attention. The dinghy, constructed of a simple wooden frame and varnished silk cloth, could not be used on open water. The sledges had been tested on Danes Island before take-off and their runners declared faulty. They were never repaired. The

components to build a simple boat. Three sledges made of wooden slats lashed together with cord. Now, that was all they had.

Andrée, Strindberg and Frænkel stepped out onto the ice at 11 minutes past eight. They had not noticed, but they were already losing their sense of time. They were not sure whether it was eight in the morning or eight in the evening, because the hazy, white light of the Arctic is unvarying. As time wore on, they would be increasingly unable to tell day from night. Standing on the ice, all they could see, in every direction, was whiteness. The horizon had blurred against the sky. Three men, with minimal knowledge of arctic conditions, had suddenly been plunged into a white nightmare.

Nobody knew where they were.

They cast no shadows.

Nils Strindberg

Salomon August Andrée

They have released the homing pigeons

MAY AND JUNE, 1897 were the driest months Sweden had seen for thirty years. In July, the rains came. During her summer holiday from the boarding school, Anna had moved with the Strindberg family to Solberga, their summer residence in the Stockholm archipelago. On the 17th July they rowed over to Vänö Island to fetch the post. The whole family had gathered in the drawing room to hear Nils' father, wholesaler Occa Strindberg, read the telegram aloud:

/ / THE BALLOON HAS TAKEN OFF FOR THE NORTH POLE / /

Anna's cheeks blushed furiously. She said nothing. Tears trickled slowly down her face. Occa comforted her and at that moment they decided, together, that they would wait a year before worrying. A year, starting that day.

But he did not say what he really thought. He felt as though he had just received word of Nils' death.

On an ice floe: 82° 38'.7 N. / 29° 40' E.

My dearest sweetest girl!

As I pick up the pen after a week's silence, to
write and speak to you, I would first beg your
forgiveness for the anxiety and grief which I
have caused you on account of the events of
this week. How many times have I not thought
of it with abhorrence, and yet I am convinced
this venture is the found   of our future
happiness. And when I return and we enjoy
the bliss of owning each other once more,
thoughts of this time will doubtless often
make us happy and make us feel even more
drawn to one another.

For several days I have studied our captain recording our journey across the Arctic, like a red slash across the white maps. When we reach the 82° 56' parallel he kills the icebreaker's engines. As the hypnotic rumbling ceases, I feel suddenly awake.

We are at the exact spot where the Eagle touched down with Andrée, Strindberg and Frænkel.
I want to stand in that spot.

The polar bear guard climbs down the ladder first with his gun. Then they let me off. And now I'm walking straight out onto the pack ice. And it holds my weight. Crap, it really holds my weight. There's no yield at all. A milky, white haze fills the air. Fine snow drifts horizontally. Everywhere, in every direction, there's whiteness. I take a few steps. I cast no shadow. It's like walking inside a cloud, and somewhere in all this whiteness the sun turns in perfect revolutions, round and round, without ever dipping toward the horizon. I take off my mittens. Push my fingers into the snow. I can't feel whether the icy crust is warm or cold. I hold on tight. Taste it. I hear myself saying, in this weird, squeaky voice: it tastes just like regular snow. What did I think it would taste like?

Somewhere at the bottom of the ocean, ten thousand feet below, sunk into the layers of sediment, lie the remains of what was once a basket of braided willow, large enough to carry three polar explorers.

WHEN THEY AWOKE ON THE MORNING of the 18th July, all the pigeons had flown away. Drizzly, almost imperceptible rain hung in the air, like mist. For four nights, the little expedition had slept side by side in the silk tent they had brought with them. They shared a three-man sleeping bag made of reindeer skin, placed directly on the thin groundsheet. They had not moved from the spot where they landed. The balloon was empty, flattened against the ice, like a large, ruddy puddle.

It is so obvious *now*, knowing what the Arctic looks like on a map, that they were in the middle of a continent consisting of nothing but ice, but to Andrée, Strindberg and Frænkel this region was still unexplored. Following the emergency landing, Andrée scaled the balloon's basket several times a day to scan the waste through his field glass. He was looking for land. Mountains. Open water. Anything.

The little camp was quiet as they methodically worked on lashing the sledges together with cord, assembling the boat and deciding what to salvage from the several tonnes of carefully packed stores brought in the Eagle. There were stackable aluminium cans and tin boxes of food, enough to feed three people for three and a half months. Nils Strindberg wrote detailed inventories of provisions and equipment. Four kinds of biscuits and readymade, tinned sponge cake. Sardines. Pemmican, which could be mixed with melted snow to make a thick gruel. The sledges had to be light enough to haul. On the other hand, they had to bring enough supplies to make it across the ice to dry land on foot. They packed and repacked for over a week. They chose carefully.

Despite Andrée's unshakable faith in the capacity of the Eagle, large wooden crates with provisions, medicine, weapons and whisky had been prepared on dry land, far to the south, to help the expedition survive a wintering. An expedition in distress could only be rescued during the summer months. By September, the Arctic Sea starts freezing over. The whole of the Arctic becomes covered in ice, and no rescue ships would be able to make their way in. The closest depot was on the Seven Islands, off the north coast of Spitsbergen, 200 miles to the south of where they landed. But they chose a different route. A larger depot had been prepared on Cape Flora on Franz Josef Land, the group of islands in the Arctic Sea where Nansen and Johansen survived a winter two years previous. Franz Josef Land was 220 miles away.

It was time to go.

Dearest fiancée!

It is nearly 7 o'cl. in the evening and we have
just finished packing our sledges and are
about to leave the site o   ur landing. Yes, we
are setting off now
at   GMT.

We shall see if we can make it to Cape Flora,
the sledges are heavy. Well, here we go...

The unceasing noise. A polar wind rebounding off nothing. The sharp creaking of massive ice floes fracturing and breaking. They carried whistles, because if they were to fall into the water, their cries for help would not be heard.

At the 1st camp site.

Well, my beloved, now your Nils knows what
it means to walk across the polar ice. We had
a slight misadventure at the outset. As we
were crossing from our ice floe the 1st sledge
ran aslant and fell into the water. We were able
to right it only with great difficulty. I stood with
water up to my knees, holding the ~~slege~~ sledge
to prevent it from sinking. Andrée and Frænkel
crossed over to the other ice floe and at length
we recovered the sledge. But my sack, which
was on that sledge, is probably wet inside,
and that is where I keep all your letters and
your portrait. Yes, ~~I~~ they will be my dearest
keepsakes this winter. Oh, my love, what will
you be thinking this winter. That is my only
concern.

EACH SLEDGE WEIGHED 440 POUNDS. It would be impossible for one person to pull something that heavy. No more than three hours into their journey, they were forced to adapt their strategy and instead move one sledge at a time, by pushing it a few hundred feet, all together. Then they would go back and do the same with the next sledge. And the next. This mode of travel made the road to dry land five times as long.

Having struggled on for four days, they repacked their sledges, abandoning a large portion of their equipment on the ice. For some reason they nevertheless kept many seemingly superfluous items, which weighed their sledges down and slowed their progress. Even though the weight of each sledge was reduced by almost 130 pounds, Fraenkel insisted on burdening himself with several encyclopaedias, including the ponderous tome *A History of the World* by A G Nathorst. They also seem to have anticipated a need for the following things: thumb tacks, cravats, a pink and white silk neckerchief. A large, white cotton table cloth decorated with embroidery and fringe. A brass grapnel anchor. Several padlocks and keys. Bottles of port and champagne.

The ice was not smooth at all, though it had seemed so from the air. In order to make any progress whatsoever, Andrée, Strindberg and Fraenkel had to take turns hewing tracks for the sledges' runners with axes and shovels. The ice sheet was under constant pressure from compression, causing the frequent formation of new ridges and cracks. Wide leads would open up suddenly, exposing the glassy, dark blue Arctic Ocean. The sea was several thousand feet deep.

LIKE TINY SPECKS OF DARK BLUE in an endless, hazy, ice waste, the three men hauled sledges that weighed far too much across hummocks, open channels and ice floes. Strindberg had written award winning essays about *the conductivity of solutions after the addition of small quantities of non-conductive materials*. Frænkel had specialist knowledge of railroad construction. Andrée had experience penning impassioned motions to the City Council on the topic of building subways underneath Stockholm in an effort to mitigate the city's unemployment levels. No one in the group knew anything about the one thing they needed now: how to survive in arctic conditions. They also knew nothing about glaciology, marine biology or marine chemistry. Nevertheless, they began collecting samples as soon as they landed, more or less at random.

Algae from blocks of ice and melt ponds were wrapped in gauze and packaged. They collected clay and sticks. The grain size composition of the clay was measured and recorded. They plucked out the eyes of a gull chick they shot so that someone at some point, someone else, with the required expertise, would be able to examine why gulls are unaffected by snow blindness. They took measurements and made drawings. Numbers were meticulously noted down in their logbooks in long, neat columns. They did and redid calculations. They held onto details, of the seemingly meaningless kind. Incredibly thorough research. Real, and yet, make-believe.

The ice is actually not white at all. With each parallel we pass on our way north, the colour of the ice changes with the light. Every morning, as I peer out the porthole in my cabin, I decide which colour will be the colour of the day. I select the swatch that most closely resembles the colour of the ice and print it on my printer. Because the boat jerks and shakes as it makes its way through the pack ice, all my things are tied down with bungee cord, to prevent them sliding and falling off shelves and tables. To print my colour swatch I have to untie the printer and hold it in my arms; parry the vibrations of the boat, otherwise the shaking causes strange pink lines to appear across the paper. I pick colours carefully. Compare it to what's outside my window. I hold the printer in my arms as the sheets of A3 rattle out onto the floor and cover my walls, day by day, with all my swatches. I make alterations and improvements. I hold onto details, of the seemingly meaningless kind. Incredibly thorough research. Real, and yet, make-believe.

Different colours have different wavelengths. Blue light has the shortest wavelength, red light the longest. If the ice looks turquoise at the eighty-fourth parallel it's because it has not absorbed the turquoise light. Ice that looks turquoise has absorbed all colours, except for turquoise. The colour of the ice is therefore not the one you can see. The ice contains all the colours you can't see.

But maybe it makes no difference: colour isn't a characteristic intrinsic to nature. Colour doesn't exist in the actual object; it is constructed in the brain of the beholder. Colour itself isn't created until someone is there to see it. Here I am, plastering the walls of my cabin with meticulously selected colour swatches. But the second I leave, they vanish.

THE 24TH JULY. Anna's twenty-sixth birthday was celebrated under an overcast sky. The Strindbergs and Anna picked wild strawberries and took the boat out. Some of the homing pigeons brought to Danes Island never boarded the balloon. Anna was given one as a present, in an iron cage. They kept it on Solberga's veranda. She named it Lakmé, after her and Nils' favourite opera. Their song.

Everyone lined up for a photograph. The birthday girl's mind was somewhere else entirely.

Anna Charlier   Occa Strindberg, Nils' father

My beautiful darling!

We have just stopped for the day after pulling and dragging our sledges for 10 hours. I am really rather tired but must exchange a few words with my beloved. First and foremost I must congratulate you. For this is the day of your birthday. Oh how I wish I could let you know that I am in the best of health and that you need not worry about us. We shall make it home in the end, you'll see.

NILS STRINDBERG CHECKED HIS CALCULATIONS. He checked them again. But the numbers were right. Determining their position on the 2nd August, he discovered that the ice they had crossed had been drifting north faster than they had walked south. Though they had no way of perceiving it, the ice sheet was in constant motion. Ice drifts. During the last few days they had spent every waking moment pulling their sledges, more than 10 hours a day, and still they had made no progress. In fact, they had retreated.

At this point Nils stopped writing to Anna.

They decided to change their course. They realised there was no chance of them reaching Franz Josef Land before winter set in. The expedition's new goal was the depot on the Seven Islands. They no longer kept track of how many times they had lost their footing and slid into the water with their sledges. The Seven Islands were 140 miles away. They hoped to reach the depot in six or seven weeks.

Six weeks later they were 14 miles closer to their destination on the Seven Islands.

THREE MEN STRUGGLED ACROSS THE PACK ICE. Even in the balloon, Nils Strindberg's feet had been cold, but his only alternative footwear, a pair of sport boots, were even colder. He kept stepping in puddles and melt ponds. His boots were filled with sodden shoe hay, which no longer insulated his damp woollen socks from the soaked shoe leather. His outfit was fashionable, recently purchased at Jaeger and Widforss and eminently suited to an elegant balloon ride, hundreds of metres above the impenetrable pack ice. Thick, black and white chequered, machine knitted socks, knee length, navy blue knickerbockers with matching vest and a bespoke woollen hunting jacket, its pockets asymmetrically placed and its satin lining both chequered and striped. The wallet in his pocket contained a token in the shape of a small silver boar. A button. Coins worth a total of 3 kronor and 5 öre. He wore thin long johns in two layers, labelled NS in cross stitch. A woollen jumper, the red stripes of which were slowly fading underneath a greasy layer of brown dirt. The damp garments were stiff with frost when he woke up in the mornings; the welts at the end of the jacket sleeves were covered in blood and blubber from the handling of seal and polar bear meat and innards. He wore the same clothes day and night.

Nils Strindberg struggled across the pack ice. A gold heart hung around his neck. The locket contained a photo of Anna and a lock of her hair. It was Friday the 4th September. It was his twenty-fifth birthday.

They walk one way.

The ice under their feet drifts

in the opposite direction.

BY SEPTEMBER THEY WERE ENCOUNTERING ice sludge. The arctic summer was all but over. The open water between the ice floes was beginning to freeze over, but because ice floes are always in motion, newly formed ice is constantly churned into a thick white gloop that will not reliably carry the full weight of a person. When the members of the expedition attempted to use the small sailcloth dinghy, the oars got stuck in the sludge. They sought passable routes through the frozen wasteland where they would be able to cross without sinking. Some days they waded through knee-deep, zero degree water. When they pulled off their boots and socks inside the tent at night, their feet were covered in blisters. On the 8th September they hauled their sledges for five hours. During those five hours they advanced just over half a mile. The next day Frænkel had such severe foot pain he was unable to continue pulling his own sledge.

So far, they had walked in the light of a midnight sun that shone bright both day and night, but now the evenings were steadily growing darker. The sun had begun to dip below the horizon. They realised they would not make it to a depot before the onset of the polar night. The state of Frænkel's and Strindberg's feet was such that they could no longer go on. They started building an ice hut to winter in, on the ice floe they happened to be on, in the middle of the pack ice. They had no other choice.

The only way of staying alive until spring was to find shelter from the approaching winter storms and hope that the food would last. They tried to ration the dry goods: *per person 75 grams daily of the now completely soaked bread*, which was stored in glass bottles filled with melted snow, or *200 grams of Mellin's food*, a type of powdered gruel. They succeeded in shooting several polar bears along their route, but their stockpile of fresh meat dwindled rapidly. When they finally managed to shoot a seal, on the 15th September, they consumed not only the meat but also the brain, liver, kidneys, lungs, colon, stomach and stomach contents. The stomach contents consisted of nothing but empty cray-fish shells. At night, polar bears stalked the campsite. They were drawn by the smell of freshly slaughtered seal.

During the final days of September they dragged all their belongings into the hut and spent their nights inside it, even though it was not finished, hoping it could afford some protection against the bears. They christened the hut *Home*. At half five in the morning, their third night in the ice hut, they were woken by a sudden change in the sounds emanating from the ice. It started as a low rumbling. It escalated to a terrible crashing. The hut was flooded with briny, light blue, freezing cold water, as the ice floe they were on suddenly snapped in half.

THREE MEN ON AN ICE FLOE drifting languidly with the currents. Beside them: the remnants of a broken, uninhabitable ice hut, which had taken them two weeks to build. The temperature was falling. There is no autumn in the Arctic, the last day of summer passes straight into winter. The storms were coming. The further south they drifted, the richer the wildlife became. During the course of 12 days they managed to shoot four ringed seals, one bearded seal and two polar bears. That secured them enough food to last until at least the end of April. Peering through his telescope as usual, Andrée suddenly spotted something at the distant horizon: a break in the straight line between ice and sky. An island.

Their ice floe appeared to have been caught in the undertows surrounding the island. As they drifted closer they observed that it seemed to consist of one big block of ice, an enormous glacier falling steeply into the sea. It was impossible to make landfall. The island was not marked on their white map. Andrée claimed it must be the island he had heard called New Iceland. Strindberg and Frænkel called it Kvitøya. Nowadays maps name it White Island.

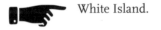 White Island.

5.
Lost.

ANNA AND OCCA STRINDBERG had agreed to wait one year before starting to worry. There was a constant stream of rumours concerning the fate of the expedition. A homing pigeon scratching for seeds on a lawn in Bedford, England. Bloodcurdling screams from a Spitsbergen cave. Three bodies, one with its skull bashed in, in a hut in northern Siberia. Not one turned out to be true.

Suddenly, in July 1898, the anniversary of the balloon launch had arrived. One year had passed. Occa and Nils' younger brother Tore moved out of the apartment on Valhallavägen 15. Anna moved in with them in their new apartment.

In the parish records from that year Nils is registered as a dependent of the household. But as the years go by, the tone of the entries changes, from the proud: *Student Nils Strindberg, member Andrée's Polar Expedition*, to: *Nils Strindberg, absent at time of registration*. The 1906 record abruptly states: *Nils Strindberg (presumed dead)*.

On a globe, we would now be underneath the round plastic disc at the top, the one you have to unscrew to change the light bulb. I can tell. Even though the world outside my cabin window is still bright white at night, it's as though someone has turned the dimmer switch down. Another half of a degree north and we will be at the North Pole. That's just over 60 miles. At the North Pole it's always every time of day at once. And if I walk in a small circle, clockwise, around the pole itself, every circuit will take me to the date line, and if I cross it I go back in time a full day. I'm looking forward to that.

One half of a degree left. We'll probably get there tomorrow. But first we have to pass the giant letters reading MADE IN TAIWAN and the enormous screw anchoring the power cord.

The North Pole 90°N

Yes it is strange to think now that we will not even be able to make it home in time for your next birthday. And perhaps we will have to spend another winter here. We do not know yet. Now our pace is so slow we may not make it to Cape Flora before winter, but will be forced to spend the dark season, like Nansen, in a hole in the ground. Poor little Anna, what despair you will feel if we do not come home next autumn. ~~But~~ And I can assure you the thought is torture to me as well, not for my own sake since I care nothing about hardships so long as I can one day come home and revel in the warmth and light of your love.

WHEN THE EXPEDITION HAD BEEN missing for the better part of ten years, Nils Strindberg was declared dead. Two years later, Anna married the Englishman Gilbert Hawtrey, a 38-year-old French teacher. They moved to America. They never had any children. A stuffed pigeon sat on a shelf in their home in New Hampshire. Under the right wing you can still make out the text, stamped across the feathers: ANDRÉE.

Anna was a piano teacher. She gave concerts. But her body had begun trembling. She wrote home to Nils Strindberg's family: *I apologise for my illegible hand, I am forced to grasp the pen with both hands to write.*

She was a concert pianist, but her hands could not stop trembling.

6.
Found.

I return from the Arctic. I failed to make it to White
Island. Yet again. I read my books, again. Go to the
museum. Again. As my children start school, I do too.
I start my medical training. Which opens up a new way
into the expedition. Now I can approach the question of
the cause of death from a medical perspective. I have to
finish what's unfinished. I speak to forensic experts,
pathologists, specialists in the fields of deficiency
disease, poisoning and exposure. I learn about symptoms
of infection and hypothermia. I return to the original
sources, scouring them for what other researchers must
have missed. I have to get inside the crumbling diaries.
I have to get inside their pockets. I have to get inside
their cells. Inside the nuclei of their cells. Inside the
double helixes of their DNA.

THE YEAR WAS 1930. Thirty-three years had passed since the Eagle took off from Danes Island. People who had been young when the Andrée expedition disappeared were now old. Young people had never heard about it.

The discovery of the expedition was a coincidence. People had long since stopped looking. White Island is a strip of glowing white in the dark green Arctic Sea northeast of Svalbard. No one would have volunteered to venture there. The few ships that did pass, at a distance, could not get near the island, because it was forever trapped in drift ice. But there was something different about the summer of 1930. It had been unusually warm, and on the 6th August a ship passed through the waters south of the island. On board M/S Bratvaag was a team of scientists, an expedition headed for Franz Josef Land. The leader of the group was geologist Gunnar Horn. To help finance the journey, they shared their vessel with a group of sealers, looking to hunt for walrus and seal on the shores along the route. As they approached White Island the fog cleared. The waters around the island were dead calm. Free of ice. For once it was possible to make landfall.

Olav Salen and Karl Tusvik were sealers. 18 and 23 years old. They had never heard of the Andrée expedition. While the older sealers got to work, skinning the newly killed walruses by the water's edge, Olav and Karl roamed the island's brown and grey beach in search of freshwater. Suddenly, a twinkling in the sand caught their eye. On one of the most remote islands of the Arctic, they found a piece of civilisation. A jar lid. The unexpected discovery made them look around more carefully. Over toward the glacier they spotted a dark silhouette against the white snow. Approaching it, they realised it was the remnants of a small rowboat, half-buried under ice. It was lashed to a sledge and laden with frozen equipment. The sealers on the shore ceased their work when excited hollering reached them over the roar of the wind. Bratvaag's skipper, Peder Eliassen, hurried up across the sand. On reaching the rowboat he picked up a boathook from the top of the pile. Rubbing the layers of ice off, he could make out the text engraved on it: ANDRÉE'S POLAR EXP. 1896. Peder Eliassen was old enough to remember the Andrée expedition.

The scientists, who had remained on the ship, were immediately brought ashore. Gunnar Horn took charge, ordering everyone not to touch anything until the area had been photographed. A few feet beyond the broken rowboat they found another sled, partly concealed beneath a layer of ice. It was empty, apart from a pair of socks, frozen crosswise to the runners. Then Peder Eliassen cried out. He had almost trod on a skeleton. On a level rock shelf, just above the sledges and the boat, he had found the body of Salomon August Andrée, who seemed to be sitting, legs outstretched, with his back against the wall. Thirty paces from that spot they found the remains of another person. Nils Strindberg was lying prone in a small crevice. His body was covered with rocks. The sealers from Bratvaag all had to pitch in to dig the two bodies out of their icy cocoons. The bodies were then carried to the ship along with the sledges, the rowboat and several hundred other items. They looked for the third member of the expedition. But Knut Frænkel was nowhere to be found.

Gunnar Horn's expedition subsequently resumed its mission. Their ship left White Island the very next day, but Horn made up his mind to return as soon as their work on Franz Josef Land had been completed. It could be that more items lay waiting under the compacted layers of ice. When they returned three weeks later, however, the island was once more impossible to reach. The waves around White Island were much too high and the waters treacherous. When they studied the beach through their binoculars they could see a polar bear prowling about the campsite.

WHEN THE SENSATIONAL NEWS of the discovery on White Island broke, one Swedish freelance journalist rented a vessel to intercept Gunnar Horn's expedition at sea for a first, exclusive interview. His name was Knut Stubbendorff. He was not the only journalist to have that idea. When he realised others would beat him to the punch, he decided to instead strike out for White Island on his own. With only one functioning engine, a radio intermittently on the blink and a reluctant crew, M/S Isbjörn voyaged across the open sea for nine days. Oblivious to his remarkable luck, Stubbendorff arrived to find ice free waters around White Island. Coming ashore on White Island, three polar bears that refused to heed the crew's warning shots had to be killed.

One month had passed since Horn's expedition left. Even more items had thawed out of the ice. The snow had melted, revealing skeletal parts from animals and humans, mittens and woollen jumpers, broken tin cans, wooden crates filled with scientific instruments from the nineteenth century. A cranium. A third sledge, its contents littering the ground around it, had appeared. Stubbendorff had brought a photographer, who documented the scene before they began collecting the items. As they were excavating the camp, stabbing at the ice with spits, the hard layers unexpectedly gave way. They had accidentally put a spit straight through Knut Frænkel's cranium. It was hard work extricating Frænkel's body from the ice. They had to shoot four more polar bears that ventured too close. Three days after its arrival, Stubbendorff's ship had to depart again, because the wind had shifted and the drift ice was closing in around White Island, turning the water into impenetrable white sludge.

Having been buried under the ice for 33 years, Andrée's, Strindberg's and Frænkel's remains were brought back to civilisation. Their equipment was retrieved. Hundreds of items, man-hauled across the ice for months on end, only to be left frozen and forgotten on Svalbard's most remote island. Detailed expedition diaries, in which we learn that their ice floe drifted around the glacial island with the currents, at length bringing them to the only place where making landfall is possible, the beach at the island's southernmost point. Nils Strindberg's sledge, one of its runners broken during their march and repaired with string. The knot he tied on the ice on the 29th August 1897 still holds. A medicine box full of pills, neatly packed in glass vials. Rolls of film with 93 pictures taken during the course of their frosty march, the 15 pound camera, which they had had to heave onto its tripod before every shoot. Nils Strindberg's almanacs, in which the life of a 24-year-old in Stockholm, before the launch, is revealed in page after frost-laminated page of diary entries: *Had some letters and wrote a letter to Anna. A merry and pleasant letter, though I do say so myself.* Columns detailing his expenses: *Book about skiing, 0.30 kr. Dinner at Opris, 2.90 kr. To a less fortunate man, 0.05 kr. Anna and I speak on the telephone every day since a phone was installed in the hallway on, I think, the 9th.* Embroidered towels. Monogrammed wool socks. A birthday letter from Nils Strindberg's younger brother: *To be opened on your birthday the 4th September*, written by a boy who did not know where Nils would be when he opened it.

A moment frozen in time. An engagement ring, wedged between the rocks of a grave.

1. Bowl
2. Primus stove and mug
3. Andrée's humerus
Centre: Andrée's remains covered by cloth.
Under the snow: Andrée's lower legs.

Strindberg's grave, the body removed

Strindberg's
cranium

Andrée's pelvis and spine

Strindberg's packing basket. Letter from Anna

ON THE FOURTH basement level of the National Library of Sweden, there is a microfilm archive with every Swedish newspaper published since 1787. It is so cold down there, blankets are provided to keep you warm while you fiddle with the reels in the microfilm readers in the dark. I scroll and read. Scroll and read. And I am cold, despite the blanket. When I go through the reports of the people who first discovered the camp in 1930, I notice that their opinions about what might have happened are at odds, to say the least.

.   ˙

˙

"All the signs suggest that Andrée and his fellow explorers must have either crashed their balloon on White Island itself or in the immediate vicinity, because the amount of luggage found there, consisting partly of non-essential items, could not have been transported any significant distance across the sea ice. Furthermore, the discovery of two polar bear pelts bearing the marks of blubber knives and a multitude of animal remains reveals that Andrée had subsisted on White Island for a considerable time. Finally, the multitude of animal remains and some unopened tin cans convince us that death was not the result of starvation. The camp was meticulously arranged with a dedicated provisions depot and a designated accommodation site outside of which the animal remains were found."

KNUT STUBBENDORFF, *Dagens Nyheter*, 7 SEP 1930

"There did not seem to be a dedicated provisions depot. Signs pointed to animals having had their way with the camp, or it may never have been properly organised in the first place."

PETER WESSEL ZAPFFE (STUBBENDORFF'S EXPEDITION), TROMSØ COUNTY COURT, 18 SEP 1930

"Judging by the appearance of the bodies when we discovered them, one can deduce that they perished from exhaustion and hypothermia. They had not had time to build any kind of shelter against the storm before succumbing. They cannot have lived long after making landfall, perhaps only a few days, possibly no more than a few hours."

GUNNAR HORN, *Dagens Nyheter*, 2 SEP 1930

"Their equipment was so abundant that fatal hypothermia can hardly be contemplated. The expedition had sufficient ammunition, rifles and food. One possibility is that they succumbed to scurvy, but this is contradicted by the fact that they had access to a mixed diet, canned foods and fresh meat."

ADOLF HOEL, GUNNAR HORN'S SUPERIOR, *Dagens Nyheter*, 8 SEP 1930

"The order at the campsite seems to have been meticulous, and the expedition appears to have suffered a sudden catastrophe, such as a blizzard."

GUNNAR HORN, *Svenska Dagbladet*, 8 SEP 1930

"The hand was bare, balled in a fist-like gesture symptomatic, according to the Arctic natives, of death from hypothermia."

KNUT STUBBENDORFF ON FRÆNKEL, *Dagens Nyheter*, 18TH SEP 1930

"It would be strange if the men had succumbed to scurvy, but no other explanation to the tragedy has been found."

DISTRICT DOCTOR BERTRAND DYBWAD-HOLMBOE, *Dagens Nyheter*, 8 SEP 1930

"One possible theory, though it is only a theory, is that the other members of the expedition [after the death of Strindberg] were poisoned by tinned food. Frænkel would then have died first, followed by Andrée."

ADOLF HOEL, *Svenska Dagbladet*, 8 SEP 1930

"It is not possible firmly to conclude that Frænkel and Andrée died at approximately the same time. Old Björvik, for example, who lives up here in Tromsø, has wintered with a dead man. He conversed with him to keep depression at bay."

ADOLF HOEL, *Dagens Nyheter*, 19 SEP 1930

ANNA HAWTREY'S MAIDEN NAME was Charlier. In 1930 she was 59 years old and resided in England. She had lived abroad for over two decades. She was on a short visit to Sweden, staying with Nils Strindberg's cousins, when news of the Andrée expedition hit.

The dead were given a lavish reception. The coffins containing the remains of the members of the expedition were transported back via Tromsø, along the Norwegian and Swedish coasts. The ship pulled in at every harbour en route, escorted by single engine planes flying low to throw wreaths into the sea as they passed. Cannons fired mourning salutes. Piers were crowded with jostling children and adults carrying binoculars. Finally brought onto Swedish soil on Skeppsholmen, in pouring rain, the coffins and the skeletal remains they contained were received by King Gustaf V. Church bells tolled throughout the city as three horse-drawn catafalques passed through the streets. A large funeral procession followed in their wake. Men in top hats and women in mourning dress and veils, moving solemnly toward Stockholm Cathedral along rain soaked cobbled streets, watched by tens of thousands of onlookers. Sweden was in mourning.

Anna did not stay for the funeral. She travelled back to her husband in England. Among the hundreds of wreaths covering the coffins in Stockholm Cathedral, there was one with an unusually simple ribbon. On the white ribbon, gold letters: *To Nils from Anna*. What else could she say? She was married to another.

(Later) We have now made camp for the night had some coffee and cheese sandwiches and bis   then biscuits and cordial and   . Andrée is   pitching the tent and Frænkel is making me   logical observations. Just now Frænk offered me a sweet, a real delicacy. There is certainly no room to be finicky here. Last night I served (because I do the housekeeping you see) a soup that really was not very good. That ~~Rosseaua Rosseauian pemmican tastes rather~~ awful one soon grows tired of it. But still it went down rather easily.

Well, we have stopped for the night in an open space, ice all around, ice in every direction. You saw that from Nansen's pictures what this kind of ice looks like hummock walls and ice leads alternating with ice fields, ever the same. We are seeing a light snowfall at the moment, but the weather is calm at least and not especially cold (-o°,8). I am sure you have pleasanter summer weather at home.

ANDRÉE HAD BEEN A MEMBER of the Swedish Cremation Society. It was a radical organisation, lobbying for the introduction of cremation in Sweden. After the funeral his remains were burnt. No one knows what Strindberg and Frænkel thought about cremation, but their coffins were burnt on the same occasion. The three urns containing the members of the Andrée expedition were placed in a shared grave at Stockholm's Northern Cemetery.

Their bodies were cremated. The clothes they wore when they died cannot be analysed for chemical residue because they have been laundered and treated too many times for any results to be conclusive. If I am to discover what they really died of, I have to locate a sample from their bodies. A piece of bone, a tissue sample or a few hairs would solve everything. With modern methods, only a small sample is needed to search for deadly levels of things like lead, copper, opium or morphine. But there are no pathology samples. There is nothing left.

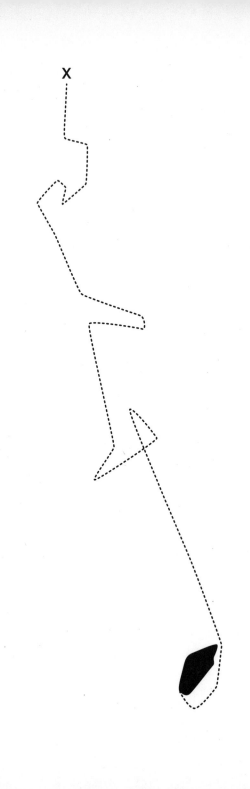

For almost fifteen years I've stalked two lovers. I'm so close now, I've almost caught up with them. I've tasted their favourite foods. I know exactly how many times they were late for class in the seventh grade. I've tried on their mittens. I've flipped through their photo albums. I've removed the photographs from the adhesive corners of the album to see what secrets they wrote on the back. I know how many steps you have to climb (78) to get to the corner apartment on the fifth and top floor in the building on Valhallavägen 15. I've stood there, my hand on the door handle. I've almost caught up.

I know their phone numbers by heart.
Nils Strindberg: 2250 (national phone line). 2090 (public phone).
Anna Charlier: Petersberg 5 (public phone).
No one picks up when I call.

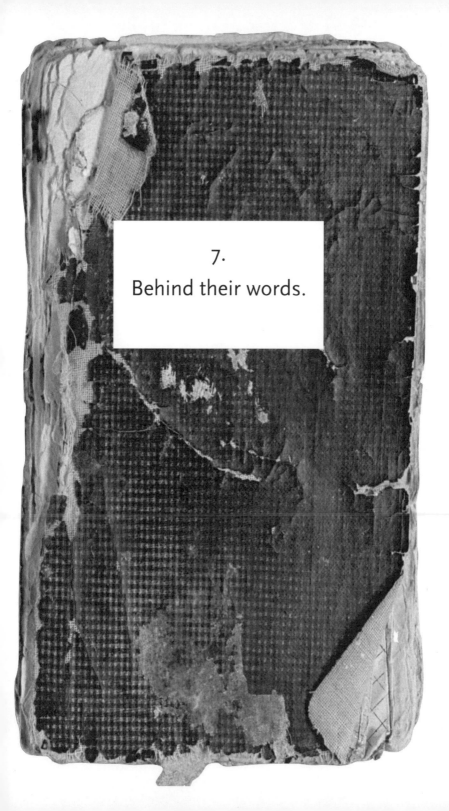

7.
Behind their words.

THE DIARIES OF THE ANDRÉE EXPEDITION are kept in a special room at the Royal Swedish Academy of Sciences, where a constant humidity of 48 per cent is maintained. They are a lot smaller than I had imagined. The diaries are full of meticulous daily notes: three men set out in a balloon. They were strong, proud and healthy. No more than a week or so after setting out, they started noticing symptoms they could not quite account for. Did they mention anything in passing, which could reveal a connection, even though they themselves did not see it? Were they already showing signs of illness during the march across the ice, signs that could explain why they died after only a few days on White Island?

I collect all the information from the different diaries, side by side for comparison. It started as a small table in my notepad. It grew. Somewhere between the handwritten lines a secret is lurking. I just have to look closely enough.

PART 1. BALLOON JOURNEY FROM DANES ISLAND

Date	Weather	Food consumption	Physical activity	Mental state
11 July 1897	Temperature +0.4° – +5.9° Wind 9 m/s Effective temperature -6° – +1° Visibility Light fog, heavier toward evening	Beer Lunch: Sandwiches, warm broth with macaroni Supper: Coffee		Strindberg: *Pleasant company* Andrée: *Spirits are high*
12 July 1897	Temperature +0.2° Wind NW – W 3.6 m/s Later dead calm Effective temperature -2° – +0.2° Precipitation Drizzle Visibility Heavy fog	They eat nothing for 17 hours Breakfast: Coffee is made Lunch: No record Supper: No record		Andrée: *Spirits are excellent. I cannot deny that a feeling of pride dominates all three of us*
13 July 1897	Temperature 0° Wind NW 2.1 m/s Effective temperature -3° Precipitation Fine drizzle leaving a layer of frost on the balloon rig Visibility Dense fog	Breakfast: No record Lunch: Potage Hotchpotch, Chataeu Briand, Kronan beer, chocolate with biscuits, biscuits with raspberry cordial and water Supper: No record		

PART 2. ON THE ICE. 82° 56' N 29° 52' E

Date	Weather	Food consumption	Physical activity	Mental state
14 July 1897	Temperature +0.2° Wind NW Precipitation 10 Visibility Altocumulus Nimbus, fairly clear air	No record (There is no shortage of provisions over the course of the next week)	The balloon's vents are opened. They land on the ice. 7 hours of hard work	

ymptoms/injuries	Medication	Miscellaneous	Comments
		Ballast is thrown overboard	They seem to have been pleased to be on their way, despite the disastrous accident at take-off, when the Eagle lost its drag ropes
		The North Pole buoy is thrown as ballast* Come evening, the balloon is hitting the ice every five minutes. At 10 p.m. the balloon stops entirely, a drag rope has been caught on a piece of ice	*Had they already realised that they would not reach the North Pole?
trindberg is rsick, vomits, s feet are cold ndrée receives a ow to the head rom what, is nknown)		The balloon remains motionless throughout the night, after 13 hours it is freed but resumes its regular collisions with the ground. Ballast is thrown Strindberg changes from boots to fur-trimmed galoshes (leather overshoes)	
red, hungry		Strindberg takes photographs of the expedition on the ice	Strindberg's photographic work suddenly changes from extroverted to introverted as he turns the camera on the expedition

Date	Weather	Food consumption	Physical activity	Mental state
15 July 1897	Temperature +0.2° Wind NW 4.4 m/s Effective temperature -4° Precipitation 10 Fine drizzle	No record	They remain in the same place	
16 July 1897	Temperature +0.25° Wind NW 3.6 m/s Effective temperature -4° Precipitation 10* [* = snow] Visibility Heavy fog	No record	They remain in the same place	Strindberg: *Good days**
17 July 1897	Temperature +0.1° Wind NW 5 m/s Effective temperature -5° Precipitation 10* Visibility Fairly good	No record	They remain in the same place	Strindberg: *Good days*
18 July 1897	Temperature +0.5° Wind NW 4.5 m/s Effective temperature -4° Precipitation 10* Visibility Fairly good	No record	They remain in the same place	Strindberg: *Good days*
19 July 1897	Temperature -1° Wind SW 4.0 m/s Effective temperature -6° Visibility Heavy fog	No record	They remain in the same place	
20 July 1897	Temperature +0.7° Wind SW 4.8 m/s Effective temperature -6° Precipitation 10*	No record	They remain in the same place	

*Are we to understand
that other days were less
good?

Inventory of provisions
sometime between the 17th
and 19th July

Andrée shoots a polar bear
(no. 1)

Date	Weather	Food consumption	Physical activity	Mental state
21 July 1897	Temperature +0.7° Wind SW 2.8 m/s Effective temperature -4° Visibility Sunshine, clouds	Polar bear (no. 1) is cooked	They remain in the same place. They load the sledges	

PART 3. MARCH ACROSS THE ICE IN THE DIRECTION OF THE DEPOT ON CAPE FLORA, FRANZ JOSE

Date	Weather	Food consumption	Physical activity	Mental state
22 July 1897	Temperature -0.6° Wind SE 4.0 m/s Effective temperature -5° Visibility Heavy fog	No record (they have plenty of food)	They set out for dry land. Their sledges are heavy. Andrée's sledge weighs 465 lbs.* Strindberg's sledge slips into the water	Strindberg: *A good sense of camaraderie*
23 July 1897	Temperature -1.5° Wind SE 2.8 m/s Effective temperature -5° Visibility Sunshine. Later on, hazy and windy	Breakfast: No record Lunch: A meagre meal Supper: Pea soup, biscuits, stock capsule, Rosseau's pemmican	The sledges are heavy. Difficult ice leads	Strindberg: *Andrée and I disagree regardir the crossing of th lead*
24 July 1897	Temperature +0.5° Wind SW 4.75 m/s Effective temperature -4° Precipitation 10* Visibility Overcast	Breakfast: No record Lunch: A meagre meal Supper: A soup that was *thoroughly unappetising* (Strindberg) made from Rosseau's pemmican, coffee, cheese sandwiches, biscuits, cordial, sweets	The sledges are heavy	Andrée: *The going was difficu and we were utterly exhausted* Strindberg: *We are now progressing so slowly that we may not reach Cape Flora this winter but may, like Nansen, have to winter ir a hollow in the ground. I am sic to think of it*
25 July 1897	Temperature +0.4° Wind S 1.1 m/s Effective temperature +0.4° Precipitation Overcast. Snow and rain throughout the night	Breakfast: Cocoa with condensed milk, biscuits and sandwiches. Cordial Lunch: No record Supper: No record	They stay in the tent half the day, dozing	Strindberg: *Spirits are excellent* Andrée: *Strindberg falls the water and w in clear mortal danger*

ymptoms/injuries	Medication	Miscellaneous	Comments
		No more than three hours into the march, they are forced to change tactics, collectively hauling one sledge at a time, because they are so heavily loaded	*On modern polar expeditions the maximum load is bodyweight x 2
hausted			Three days into the march across the ice, Andrée is already concerned about the durability of the sledges
		Anna Charlier turns 26. Two polar bears (a female with cub) visit the camp during the night.* No polar bear is shot	*Modern expeditions employ both warning fences and dogs to protect against polar bears

Date	Weather	Food consumption	Physical activity	Mental state
26 July 1897	Temperature +0.4° Wind N 1.5 m/s Effective temperature -1° Precipitation 10. It is raining when they wake up at 12 noon Visibility Heavy fog	Breakfast: Cocoa with condensed milk, biscuits and sandwiches Lunch: Polar bear steak Andrée: *Bear steak splendid. The meat left in sea water for 1 hour** Supper: No record	Sedentary, they stay in the tent, dozing. The sledges are repacked	Andrée: *Northerly winds, hurrah.* (The wind has finally shifted to the north.) *Strange emotions and culinary excesses during reduction* (Food and equipment was left on the ice.)
27 July 1897	Temperature -1° Wind NW 5.75 m/s Effective temperature -7° Precipitation 10* Strong winds	Polar bear meat. Pemmican reduced. Larger bread rations. That evening supper is taken inside the tent: champagne,* biscuits with honey	Andrée: *An exceedingly laborious day's worth of work, particularly for F.*	Andrée: *Even Frænkel complained of fatigue***
28 July 1897	Temperature -1.8° Wind NW 4.4 m/s Effective temperature -7° Visibility Fog	Polar bear meat	Marching. The snow shoes are broken in. 16 hour march across the ice	
29 July 1897	Temperature 0° Wind N 1.9 m/s Effective temperature -2° Precipitation 10 Visibility Altocumulus Heavy fog	Polar bear meat	Marching across the ice	

ymptoms/injuries	Medication	Miscellaneous	Comments
		Until this date the three men have hauled one sledge at a time, doubling back to haul the next and so on. The sledges are reorganised – they pack provisions to last them 45 days. Strindberg shoots a polar bear (no. 2)	*A cooking method that was in vogue during the end of the 19th century according to gastronomic researchers. They realise their heavy sledges are impeding their progress too much
rænkel fatigue		Frænkel shoots a polar bear (no. 3) Andrée's sledge now weighs 285.5 lbs Frænkel's sledge: 318.8 lbs Frænkel's sledge breaks (after 6 days' use) and is repaired	Despite lightening the sledges' load and resting all of the previous day, they are tired. Of the members of the expedition, Frænkel was considered to be in best physical condition. Is he already weakened by illness? *The bottle of champagne they brought is sacrificed here! **Andree and Strindberg must have complained of fatigue previously
		Andree: *The wind was bitingly cold.* The sledges have to be looked at and reinforced	The coldest day so far

Date	Weather	Food consumption	Physical activity	Mental state
30 July 1897	Temperature +0.8° Wind N 6 m/s Effective temperature -4° Precipitation 10. Rain throughout the night Visibility Fog	Andrée regarding the daily routines: *Bear steak now twice daily* Frænkel makes sandwiches	Marching across the ice Andrée falls in the water	Andrée: *A particularly wearying day* Completely exhausted at bedtime
31 July 1897	Temperature +0.6° Wind N 3.5 m/s Effective temperature -3° Visibility Fog	Polar bear meat twice daily	Walking on their knees through deep snow. Strindberg falls in the water	Andrée (regarding the drifting of the ice): *It is not encouraging.* (Regarding the group) *Spirits and mood are excellent.* Strindberg writes a final letter to Anna, but stops halfway through
1 August 1897	Temperature +0.5° Wind NW 3.8 m/s Effective temperature -4° Precipitation 1 Visibility Cirrostratus Very heavy fog	Running out of polar bear meat	Strindberg: *Good march 5 miles*	
2 August 1897	Temperature -0.4° Wind N 1.9 m/s Later on: dead calm Effective temperature -3° – -0.4° Precipitation 10 Visibility Cirrostratus	The last of the polar bear meat is eaten. New polar bear shot: from this they take not only the meat but also the fillet from the back and one kidney (1.1 lbs.), the tongue and ribs Andrée: *Old worn-out male with worm-eaten teeth*	Exceedingly difficult terrain	They are more tired than usual when they wake up, despite easy terrain the previous day

ymptoms/injuries	Medication	Miscellaneous	Comments
rænkel xperiences the rst symptoms of now blindness		Shoe impregnation is usually the first order of the day*	Snow blindness or symptoms of some disease/infection? According to Tryde (the man with the trichinosis theory) snow blindness is one of the first signs of trichinosis
			*Their shoes are already wet due to ground condition
		That evening's astronomical position determination reveals that the ice has drifted west faster than they have walked east	The last letter from Nils to Anna
		Despite walking south, they drift north with the ice	*So their feet are wet
		Andrée: *The drying of socks is best done by wearing them on one's feet, outside one's woollen socks**	
		Strindberg: *Summer day*	One of the warmest days so far – no chill factor
		Andrée: *Clear, calm and hot all day*	They have taken to eating both tongue and kidney of polar bear
		New polar bear (no. 4) shot by Andrée	

Date	Weather	Food consumption	Physical activity	Mental state
3 August 1897	Temperature +0.4° Wind E 0.35 m/s Effective temperature +0.4° Visibility Fog by the horizon The previous night it was too hot in the tent; the sun is shining (midnight sun) and there is hardly any wind	Polar bear meat. Andrée (regarding the polar bear): ... *tough like leather galoshes*	Marching across the ice. Ice dreadful	Andrée: *A lot of lampooning abou my old bear, which has been declared by F. to be the oldest in the polar region*
4 August 1897	Temperature -2.2° Wind 1.25 m/s Effective temperature -2.2° Visibility Cirrostratus Altocumulus Precipitation 6	Breakfast: Polar bear steaks with hard bread, lactoserin chocolate [nutritionally enhanced chocolate drink] with biscuits Lunch: Biscuits, butter, cheese, meltwater	12 hour march across the ice	

PART 4. MARCH ACROSS THE ICE WITH NEW COURSE FOR THE SEVEN ISLANDS (WHERE A SMALLE

Date	Weather	Food consumption	Physical activity	Mental state
5 August 1897	Temperature -2.2° Wind NW 2 m/s Effective temperature -5° Visibility Fog at the horizon	Supper: Polar bear broth with Potage d'Oiselle (Stauffer), sandwiches, biscuits, cherry cordial and water Breakfast: Various polar bear cuts (ribs, chops and kidney), 4 pieces of bread, coffee with biscuits (6 pcs), milk	They are forced to crawl on all fours because the ice is so impassable	Andrée: *Difficult day today*
6 August 1897	Temperature +0.8° Wind NW 1.8 m/s Effective temperature -1° Visibility Overcast, heavy fog	Lunch: Biscuits (7), bread (8), butter, water Supper: Polar bear meat, various cuts 1.6 lbs, (polar bear ribs and tongue), bread and biscuits, Mellin's food gruel Breakfast: Polar bear meat, various cuts 1.7 lbs., bread (2), coffee with biscuits (6 pcs)	14–15 hour march across the ice. The snow is difficult. They slip and the sledges' runners cut deep into the snow. The sledges overturn	Fraenkel makes jokes

Symptoms/injuries	Medication	Miscellaneous	Comments
		It is so warm they do not wear their jackets while hauling. The weather also allows them to mass dry clothes. On this day they eat their food "outside", i.e. not in the tent	The warmest day so far. It is so warm they can dry their clothes. Compared to Nansen's trek across the ice: at -13° Nansen finds sleeping in the tent taxing on account of the heat
		Biscuits and bread soaked through They change course when they discover that the ice is drifting in the wrong direction Andrée: ... *agree to set our new course for the Seven Islands, which we hope to reach in 6 to 7 weeks**_	* The Seven Islands are 137 miles away. 6 weeks after this date they have only progressed 14 miles toward their destination
TED)			
		Inventory of provisions indicate that they have to be economical, especially with bread Andrée: *Temp falling lower and lower and for every night degree we crawl deeper into the sleeping bag*	
Andrée: *Our footing is unsure and we slip often* Andrée: *We are very tired, now that we have gone to bed*			Andrée: *The wind blows almost directly in our faces and has probably pushed us back just as far* Andrée: *The bear meat is very good now that it is old*

Date	Weather	Food consumption	Physical activity	Mental state
7 August 1897	Temperature 0° Wind SV 4 m/s Effective temperature -4° Precipitation 10* Visibility Fog	Lunch (at night): 4 rolls of bread and 7 buttered biscuits each, water Supper (in the morning): 2.2 lbs. polar bear meat, puree of peas (Stauffer), bread and biscuits	Marching across the ice	
8 August 1897	Temperature -0.4° Wind SW 5.1 m/s Effective temperature -5° Visibility Fog	Breakfast: 0.6 lbs polar bear steaks and 6 biscuits each, lactoserin cocoa Lunch: Regular bread ration, butter, cheese and cakes Supper: 0.9 lbs of polar bear meat each, gruel (Mellin's) + biscuits, 2 pieces of bread each	Marching across the ice. Ice fairly good	Jokes about reindeer hair (from the sleeping bag) in their food
9 August 1897	Temperature -0.9° Wind SW 4.6 m/s Effective temperature -6° Visibility Fog at the horizon	Breakfast: Polar bear meat, 0.6 lbs each with 2 rolls of bread. Coffee made from new coffee, used grounds and 2.6 pints of water + a bit of milk. Biscuits (6 pcs), milk Lunch: Bread, biscuits, butter, cheese Supper: Cloetta pemmican, chocolate, bread, biscuits and butter	18 hour march across the ice. Atrocious terrain. Their shoes get soaked	Andrée: *A marvellously beautiful bear approached us but ran away. We were sorry for it, because we are running out of bear meat*
10 August 1897	Temperature +1.2° Wind SW 3 m/s Effective temperature -2° Precipitation 10 Visibility Altocumulus	Breakfast: Polar bear meat, bread, Mellin's Food gruel Lunch: Buttered hard bread, sardines, biscuits with cheese Supper: 1.6 lbs of polar bear meat with Batty's sauce [a cold, sweet dessert sauce], broth with biscuits, almond cake Stauffer	Wearying march across the ice. The terrain is exceptionally difficult Andrée: *We have set up camp after only 7 hours of walking, but they were so very tiring*	Andrée: *We have celebrated crossing the 82nd parallel*

Symptoms/injuries	Medication	Miscellaneous	Comments
Andrée: ... *we finally awoke and felt completely rested**		Later that day they realise they are making no progress and that they have to change course yet again	*So it must have been a long time since they felt that way
Warm (at least Andrée) Andrée: *All our noses are constantly running. Permanent catarrh**		Andrée wishes he had brought a summer jacket Andrée mentions that he does not use sunglasses in strong sunshine. Instead he squints	Andrée is warm despite freezing temperatures and 5 m/s winds. It is probably easier to keep warm now that the ice is more passable and they do not need to stop constantly *Are the runny noses due to the wind or illness? It must have been affecting them for at least a couple of days
Everyone is exhausted. Frænkel has diarrhoea Andrée: *Frænkel has diarrhoea for the 2nd time and little seems to remain of his moral strength**	Frænkel opium	Strindberg's rifle is malfunctioning, they work for several hours to repair it They are running out of polar bear meat Ice sludge	When did Frænkel first suffer from diarrhoea? It is not mentioned in the diaries *Subtext! What does he mean by this? Sludge means wet feet
Frænkel's stomach complaints are cured		Inventory of sledges. Andrée's sledge weighs 295.8 lbs Strindberg's weighs 310.8 lbs. Frænkel's weighs 339 lbs.. 53 lbs are removed from Frænkel's sledge Adjustment of course once more	Thus far Frænkel has hauled a much heavier sledge then the others

Date	Weather	Food consumption	Physical activity	Mental state
11 August 1897	Temperature -1.6° Wind SW 3.0 m/s Effective temperature -5 Visibility Fog at the horizon, clear sky	Breakfast: Polar bear meat, bread, coffee, biscuits Lunch: Bread, butter, biscuits, cheese	Andrée falls in the water. Strindberg collides with Frænkel's sledge, breaks the boat	Andrée: *By the time evening was falling we were feeling distinctly unhappy*
12 August 1897	Temperature -1.6° Wind SW 4.1 m/s Effective temperature -6° Visibility Fog	Supper: 1.6 lbs of polar bear meat, lactoserin cocoa Breakfast: 1.6 lbs of polar bear meat, ivory gull shot by Frankel on the 11th August (*tasty*), Mellin's food gruel Lunch: Bread, butter, biscuits, cheese	Terrain somewhat improved, shorter march than usual	
13 August 1897	Temperature +0.7° Wind W 1.85 m/s Effective temperature -1° Precipitation 10*	Supper: 1.1 lbs of polar bear meat, two pieces of bread each, Potageau Carfeuil Stauffer with biscuits (6 each) Breakfast: 1.1 lbs of polar bear meat (final rations), 2 pieces of hard bread, coffee with biscuits Lunch: Bread, butter, sardines, cheese, cakes	Field dressing and flensing cut the march unusually short	Andree (regarding the bears they have shot): *There was much rejoicing in the caravan*
14 August 1897	Temperature -1.6° Wind S 2.1 m/s Effective temperature -4° Precipitation 10*	Supper: Fresh polar bear meat, heart, brain (3.3 lbs), ribs. Polar bear broth with meat, also bread and wheat meal biscuits Breakfast: Various fried meats: polar bear meat, ribs, heart, brain, kidneys and ivory gull (bread), coffee with wheat meal biscuits		

Symptoms/injuries	Medication	Miscellaneous	Comments
		Frænkel shoots an ivory gull	*They have been told of an island called Gillis Land, an island that does not exist
		For a moment Frænkel believes he has sighted land. (They are on the look out for Gillis Land*)	
		This day too they expect to spot Gillis Land through their field glasses	
		Only one meal's worth of polar bear meat remains; they try to shoot seal	
		Andrée shoots an ivory gull. A female polar bear (no 5) and two cubs (no 6 and 7) are shot by all three men	They now have 92.6 lbs. of polar bear meat, which has to last for 23 days. They calculate rations of 1.3 lbs. of polar bear meat per person, per day
		Andrée (regarding polar bear): ...*we found heart, brain and kidneys* to some extent *exceedingly palatable. The tongue too is well worth taking. The meat on the ribs is excellent.*	
		Andree's boots are being cut to ribbons by the icy ground	
		Andrée: *The sow stiffened quickly* (after death), *but the cubs stayed supple for a long time*	They eat large quantities of polar bear meat. By now they are also consuming polar bear brain, heart and kidneys

Date	Weather	Food consumption	Physical activity	Mental state
15 August 1897	Temperature +0.4° Wind SE 4 m/s Effective temperature -4° Precipitation Rain	Lunch: Coffee with butter, bread and biscuits Supper: Various polar bear cuts (3.3 lbs) and polar bear broth with boiled meat, bread and biscuits Andrée: *Consuming a lot of meat*	They spend this day in the tent due to the heavy rain. In addition, they need to repair their equipment	
16 August 1897	Temperature -3.4° Wind NW 5.9 m/s Effective temperature -10° Precipitation 10* Visibility Light fog, heavier toward evening	Polar bear meat		
17 August 1897	Temperature +0.2° Wind NW 3.8 m/s Effective temperature -4° Precipitation 10* Visibility Light fog, heavier toward evening	Andrée: ~~The meat from~~ *bear heart (fried) tastes a little bitter. Fried bear meat in Stauffer soup is delicious*	Marching across the ice. Rain and wind at outset. Terrain very difficult Andrée: *Our journey today has been dreadful. We have not progressed 1000 yards*	
18 August 1897	Temperature -0.8° Wind NW 1.7 m/s Effective temperature -3° Precipitation 10* Visibility It clears up for a while around 11am	The meat ration is increased to 2.4 lbs. per person Brain, kidneys, tongue and a few back cuts, around 22 lbs, are taken from the new polar bear	Marching across the ice. Terrain extremely difficult. They are forced to load the sledges onto the boat to cross leads in the ice nine times	When Andrée is sitting in the tent, mending his long johns, he does not stop sewing when he spots a polar bear through the flap; he simply says: *Would you look at that, another bear.*

Symptoms/injuries	Medication	Miscellaneous	Comments
Andrée diarrhoea, Strindberg diarrhoea, Strindberg has cut his hand and has an abscess on his upper lip	Andrée opium, Strindberg opium, Strindberg's abscess is cleaned with calomel solution	They mend the sleeping bag, their oilskins and sunglasses. Andrée fashions a raincoat They consume large quantities of polar bear meat as well as other parts of the polar bear	They have digestive problems and take opium, but this is not cited as the reason why they spend the whole day in the tent – instead they mention rain and repairs Is Strindberg's diarrhoea caused by bacterial gastroenteritis – has the meat made him ill? Strindberg's abscess is a possible entry point for bacteria, which can lead to sepsis
			They likely spend this day in the tent as well. The coldest day so far
		When the weather clears temporarily, they scan the horizon for land. They realise that they must adjust their course yet again	Despite walking all day they have not progressed even 1000 yards
		They have brought their rifles into the tent to clean them* Frænkel shoots a polar bear (no. 8), a male Andrée: *We must be approaching the seat* The sight has come loose and fallen off Frænkel's rifle, but is found and reclaimed	Yet again they demonstrate their ignorance of how dangerous polar bears are to humans *So under normal circumstances they store the rifles outside the tent. To avoid condensation and the formation of ice inside the barrels? That is routine on modern polar expeditions

Date	Weather	Food consumption	Physical activity	Mental state
19 August 1897	Temperature -0.8° Wind N 3.6 m/s Effective temperature -5° Precipitation 10*	2.4 lbs of polar bear meat per person 18 lbs. of meat from the new polar bear is loaded onto the sledges	A roughly 3 mile march across the ice. Terrain very wearying	Andrée: *Recognisance is done by me and is very strenuous. S. and F. sit waiting and get cold*
20 August 1897	Temperature -1.8° Wind N 5.4 m/s Effective temperature -7° Visibility Fog	The meat ration is increased: 2.6 lbs. for breakfast and 0.6 for lunch	Marching across the ice	
21 August 1897	Temperature -3.5° Wind N 2.2 m/s Effective temperature -7°	Polar bear meat: 2.6 lbs for breakfast and 0.6 lbs for lunch. On this day they start eating raw polar bear meat, raw kidney, raw brain, kidney tallow. Blood pancake of polar bear blood, oat flour and butter 2/3 of the tongue, the kidneys and the brains (as well as cuts from the back according to Strindberg) are taken from the new polar bears. The blood is collected The following dishes are mentioned on the 21st, but were probably not prepared on that day: algae soup, made from algae found at the edge of the ice. Loaf made from Mellin's food, dry yeast and fresh water	Marching across the ice. Difficult terrain. Their feet get soaked Andrée: *The semi-frozen leads and the fallings in have cost us an enormous amount of time*	Andrée: *Beautiful day. Clear air* Strindberg: *3 bears just now at the tent door, of which one escaped though wounded.* I dropped the mother with one shot*
22 August 1897	Temperature -4° Wind S 1.25 m/s Effective temperature -4° Visibility Heavy fog	Polar bear ham, several days old Andrée: *The polar bear ham, several days old, tasted heavenly*	Marching across the ice Andrée: *Terrible terrain*	Andrée: *The day has been perfectly beautiful. Possibly the most beautiful we have had*

Symptoms/injuries	Medication	Miscellaneous	Comments
Andrée: *Today's work has done me in completely*			*Subtext: Can we infer that Andrée feels that he is doing more work than the others, that they just sit around getting cold? Are Strindberg and Frænkel too tired to be proactive?
		2 polar bears are shot, one female (no. 9) and one cub (no 10.), by Frænkel and Strindberg Andrée: *Raw kidney with salt tastes like oysters and we had no desire to fry it. Raw brain is also very good and the bear meat can easily be eaten uncooked*	*This could be interpreted as Strindberg disparaging Andrée (for wounding a cub that escapes). The polar bears are very intrusive! Strindberg's rifle is fully functional again Wet feet "Kidney tallow" is the perinephral fat surrounding the kidney
Frænkel's foot hurts, Andrée massages it. One of Strindberg toes hurts, cause unknown (according to Andrée)		Andrée shoots an ivory gull fledgling. Andrée: *I massaged F's foot. He pulled so hard he dislocated his knee, but it slipped back in place. But it did not do any (major) lasting damage*	If Strindberg does not know why his toe is hurting, it cannot be because of chafing. Infection? Was Frænkel's knee dislocated? (Only high impact trauma can dislocate a knee). And why does Frænkel "pull", was it a spasm? What kind of foot pain is alleviated by massage – a sprain? Muscle soreness?

Date	Weather	Food consumption	Physical activity	Mental state
23 August 1897	Temperature -0.2° Wind S 5.3 m/s Effective temperature -5°	Algae soup with a large helping of algae, fried polar bear meat and a couple of spoons of Mellin's food. Bread rations are decreased to 2.6 oz hard bread and 5.3 oz biscuits. The meat rations are increased to 6.2 – 6.6 lbs. per day (i.e. 2.2 lbs per person)	A 4 mile march across the ice. The ice on the meltwater ponds is becoming more solid, but conditions are nevertheless atrocious	
24 August 1897	Temperature +1.2° Wind S 8.6 m/s Effective temperature -5° Precipitation 10	Polar bear meat: breakfast 2.8 lbs per person, 0.8 lbs for lunch. Bread: 2.6 oz per person. Biscuits: 5.3 oz per person. Butter is now only consumed with lunch (rationing)	Terrible ice conditions	
25 August 1897	Temperature +0.2° Wind S 6.0 m/s Effective temperature -5°	Polar bear meat, bread, biscuits	Ice much improved. Good distance covered despite ailments Frænkel falls in the water	
26 August 1897	Temperature +1° Wind N2.1 m/s Effective temperature -1° Visibility Altocumulus	Polar bear meat, bread, biscuits		
27 August 1897	Temperature -1.2° Wind N 1.9 m/s Effective temperature -4° Visibility Fog	Polar bear meat. Bread rations: 4 slices Schumacher bread and 6 Albert biscuits each. They now use Mellin's food in their coffee and chocolate (lactoserin cocoa)	A 4 mile march across the ice	Andrée: *One of the best days we have had. The weather has been delightful*

Symptoms/injuries	Medication	Miscellaneous	Comments
Andrée: *We are terribly tired*		Samples of the soup algae were found on White Island and are stored at the Andrée Museum Andrée (regarding the increased meat ration): *We are very happy with our diet**	They cook algae soup for the first time (cf. 21st Aug). After eating this soup they had diarrhoea for 4 straight days! They have also increased their meat rations *Does this mean that they no longer have diarrhoea or that they cannot see the connection?
Frænkel severe diarrhoea + cramps, possibly due to overexertion, Strindberg cramps.* Foot pain gone		Andrée: *F. had terrible diarrhoea last night but this was probably caused by hypothermia. He suffers from cramps, possibly due to overexertion. S-g has cured his sore foot by coating his sock with boot grease. The cramps* are instantly alleviated when massaged*	Hypothermia does not cause diarrhoea. What pain can be alleviated by spreading boot grease on one's sock? *P O Sundman believes Andrée's notes mean that both Strindberg and Frænkel suffered cramps. I am less sure
Frænkel diarrhoea Andrée diarrhoea Strindberg foot pains		Andrée shoots a small auk (bird) Inventory of provisions	
Frænkel diarrhoea			
Frænkel severe diarrhoea Andrée diarrhoea	Frænkel opium	Andrée: *F. has once again had terrible diarrhoea and hav has been given opium. I have also had diarrhoea today, but am now well again without medication**	*Subtext: Did Andrée consider Frænkel weak for requiring drugs?

Date	Weather	Food consumption	Physical activity	Mental state
28 August 1897	Temperature -5.5° Wind NW 6.8 m/s Effective temperature -13° Precipitation 10 Visibility Stratocumulus	Polar bear meat, bread, biscuits	Marching across the ice. It is now possible to cross the frozen melt ponds Andrée: *Dreadful ice*	Andrée is concerned that Fraenkel keeps falling ill: *Let's see if he mans up again*
29 August 1897	Temperature -3° Wind NW 3.5 m/s Effective temperature -8° Precipitation 1 Visibility Stratocumulus	Polar bear meat, bread, biscuits	Marching across the ice. Difficult terrain. The ice and snow are as hard as glass	Andrée: *Tonight was the first time I thought about the wonderful things they have at home. S. and F. have, by contrast, spoken about this for a long time now**
30 August 1897	Temperature -6.6° Wind NW 5.25 m/s Effective temperature -13° Precipitation 9	Polar bear meat (66 lbs are taken from the new polar bear)	The ice was much improved today. Good distance covered despite illnesses	
31 August 1897	Temperature -4° Wind NW 6.5 m/s Effective temperature -11° Precipitation 10*	Polar bear meat, bread, biscuits	Marching across the ice. Terrain fairly good	
1 Sep 1897	Temperature -3.4° Wind NW 6.9 m/s Effective temperature -10°	Polar bear meat, as well as sandwiches and coffee (to celebrate that they've managed to travel south)	Resting in the tent	Andrée: *The mood was first-rate* (as a result of the ice drifting in the right direction)
2nd Sep 1897	Temperature -5.8° Wind NW 4.2 m/s Effective temperature -12° Precipitation 8		A roughly 8 hour long march across the ice	Andrée: *The wind has now [...] un-fortunately turned S 60° W, but is thankfully not too strong*

Symptoms/injuries	Medication	Miscellaneous	Comments
Frænkel stomach pains	Frænkel morphine	Andrée: *F. is poorly again. Yesterday he was given a square of opium for the diarrhoea and tonight a square of morphine against his stomach pains**	The arctic winter looms *Opium is no longer enough on its own
		The inside of the tent is now permanently ice covered They spot a polar bear which disappears in the distance Strindberg's sledge breaks and repairs only make it just about serviceable	*Andrée starts feeling homesick. Have Strindberg and Frænkel spoken about wanting to go home a lot? Does Andrée find that trying?
		Polar bear (no. 11) shot by Frænkel. The bear is stopped only 10 paces from Strindberg They estimate that their meat stores will last for 14 days. The meat is carried underneath their clothes to prevent it from freezing*	Once again they demonstrate a lack of understanding of the fact that polar bears can attack people *This raises the temperature of the meat, boosting bacteria growth
Andrée severe diarrhoea, stomach pains, cold symptoms	Andrée morphine and opium	Andree: *The sun touched the horizon at midnight. Set the landscape alight. The snow a sea of fire* Frænkel's sledge badly broken*	Andrée believes his diarrhoea is a symptom of a cold. That is not possible The midnight sun is almost gone, the polar night is coming *Strindberg's sledge broke just a few days previous
		Andrée: *... We felt a need for rest and repairs*	Do they still suffer from diarrhoea and stomach pains or are they simply tired? Cf. comment on the 15th August
Andrée diarrhoea that night		Andrée wears woollen socks to bed for the first time	So they did not wear shoes in the sleeping bag

Date	Weather	Food consumption	Physical activity	Mental state
3 Sep 1897	Temperature -2.4° Wind SW 2.6 m/s Effective temperature -6° Precipitation 10	2.6 oz Borosimé chocolate mixed with 10 cups of water and 3.5 oz of biscuit mush (Congo biscuits)	For the first time the boat was used with all three sledges on board, rather than just for ferrying one sledge at a time across leads. 3 hours of rowing. Then a 4.5 hour march across the ice	Andrée: *This neverending hauling [...] has become a little tedious lately*
4 Sep 1897	Temperature -0.3° Wind NW 3.2 m/s Effective temperature -4°	Breakfast: Polar bear steak with bread and Stauffer pea soup with polar bear meat and bear fat Lunch: Fried polar bear meat kept warm inside their vests Supper: Polar bear meat. Bread with foie gras, Stauffer cake with raspberry syrup, water, lactoserin chocolate	Strindberg falls in the water. Only 3 hours of marching across the ice due to the time required to dry everything	A day of celebration Andrée: *We were merry and friendly as usual*
5 Sep 1897	Temperature +3.8° Wind W 1.3 m/s Effective temperature +3.8° Precipitation 10	Strindberg makes this note sometime between the 5th and 13th Sep: *We alternated between these dishes during the rest of our journey. Bear meat, kidneys, brain, back cuts, blood pancake (made from bear blood, oat flour, butter), pancake made from Mellin's food*	Extremely heavy going. A wearying 4 hour march across the ice. Then rowing	Andrée (regarding the rowing): *Exceedingly refreshing to be able to choose to travel by this method*
6 Sep 1897	Temperature -2.3° Wind SE 1 m/s Effective temperature -2.3° Precipitation 9 Visibility Heavy fog	Polar bear meat	Ice sludge, difficult to row through, difficult to walk on	
7 Sep 1897	Temperature -3.2° Wind SE 4.8 m/s Effective temperature -9° Visibility Clear	Polar bear meat	Terrible ice sludge	

Symptoms/injuries	Medication	Miscellaneous	Comments
Andrée diarrhoea		Polar bear in the camp during the night (it is not shot) Frænkel shoots a bird (probably a tystie) Andrée (regarding the tastiest parts of the bear): *The brain, the kidneys, not to mention the kidney tallow and blood pancake*	Biscuit mush = biscuits that have partially dissolved after accidental soaking
Andrée constipation		Strindberg turns 25. Andrée is cold in the sleeping bag on the night between the 3rd and the 4th of Sep: *Last night I had a single blanket instead of a double but found that cool enough* The bread, biscuits and sugar has been soaked. "Biscuit mush" is mixed with cold water and boiled with chocolate	Did Andrée take opium for his diarrhoea on the 3rd September, which in turn led to constipation on the 4th September?
Andrée constipation		Frænkel kills three ivory gulls with one shot A polar bear is spotted near the camp during the night (not shot)	
Andrée, constipation Frænkel's left foot may have given him trouble			Ice sludge can cause trench foot, a symptom of exposure that is sometimes fatal
Frænkel's left foot hurts Andrée constipation		Long and refreshing sleep. They see a walrus	

Date	Weather	Food consumption	Physical activity	Mental state
8 Sep 1897	Temperature -2.3° Wind 6.6 m/s Effective temperature -9° Precipitation 10*	They are running out of polar bear meat	A 5 hour march across the ice has brought them 1000 yards closer to their destination	
9 Sep 1897	Temperature -3.9° Wind SE 4.9 m/s Effective temperature -10° Precipitation 10*	They have almost run out of polar bear meat	Strindberg and Andrée take turns going back for Frænkel's sledge Andrée: *The terrain is inordinately difficult. It is draining* Andrée: *6 hours of walking was all we could manage* Andrée falls in the water More ice sludge	
10 Sep 1897	Temperature -1.9° Wind NE 3.5 m/s Effective temperature -6° Precipitation 10* Visibility Heavy fog			
11 Sep 1897	Temperature -4.2° Wind 5.9 m/s Effective temperature -11°			

Symptoms/injuries	Medication	Miscellaneous	Comments
Frænkel's left foot hurts			
Frænkel's left foot now hurts enough to prevent him from pulling his sledge, he is reduced to helping the others by pushing from behind Abscess is lanced Andrée: *Our diarrhoea seems to have [come to an end] ceased* [he moves his bowels often and the excrement [seems] appears to be fairly loose*, but he does not complain of stomach pains in his hitherto usual manner***	Frænkel liniment, the abscess is washed with calomel solution	Andrée kills two ivory gulls with one shot Andrée (regarding Frænkel): *I massage him morning and evening and apply the liniment. Today [...] I have lanced a large abscess, washed it with calomel solution and bandaged it*	Frænkel's abscess is a possible entry point for bacteria, which can lead to sepsis *So Frænkel has often had diarrhoea before this day **Apparently he has also had stomach pains more or less constantly Even though Andrée does not spell it out, Frænkel must at this point be struggling with his injured foot and diarrhoea
The state of Frænkel's foot is such that he can no longer pull his sledge at all One of Strindberg's feet is also *a little out of sorts*		They are now drifting north despite north-easterly winds No entries from Andrée or Strindberg	
Frænkel's foot injured. He cannot pull his sledge Strindberg's foot *out of sorts*		They drift north No entries from Andrée or Strindberg	

Date	Weather	Food consumption	Physical activity	Mental state
12 Sep 1897	Temperature -8.9° Wind NW 7.6 m/s later 10.2 m/s Effective temperature -18° – -19°		According to Andrée: *Staying put starting today on account of raging storm* According to Strindberg: *Staying put starting the day after*	

PART 5. STAYING PUT ON AN ICE FLOE. THEY BUILD A HUT TO WINTER IN

Date	Weather	Food consumption	Physical activity	Mental state
13 Sep 1897	Wind NW 12–15 m/s Precipitation*	Food rationing: 7 oz Mellin's food or 2.6 oz bread soaked in water or similar. 0.8 lbs of meat, two hot beverages daily made from 1 oz coffee, 1 oz lactoserin cocoa, 1.4 oz Stauffer powder and 2 stock capsules	They stay put due to the wind and snow	Andrée: *...when we eventually realised the necessity of facing the inevitable, i.e. to winter on the ice. Our position is not particularly good*
14 Sep 1897	Temperature -2.7° Wind NW 9.4 m/s Effective temperature -10° Precipitation 10*	Food rationing. They have almost run out of polar bear meat	They stay put on an ice floe	
15 Sep 1897	Temperature -3.8° Wind NW 7.1 m/s Effective temperature -11° Precipitation 10	Andrée: *We eat every part of the seal except for the skin and bones. The stomach and its contents as well as the intestines and liver are no exceptions. The stomach contents consisted almost exclusively of empty crayfish shells*	They stay put on an ice floe	They are concerned about the food situation Andrée: *If only we could shoot two dozen seals or so, we could be saved*
16 Sep 1897	Temperature -5° Wind W 6... Effective temperature -12° Precipitation 10*	Seal, they eat everything except the skin and bones	They stay put on the ice floe	

Symptoms/injuries	Medication	Miscellaneous	Comments
...ænkel's foot ...jured.		They keep drifting north until noon despite north-westerly winds	It is getting cold!
...trindberg's foot ...out of sorts		No entries from Andrée or Strindberg	
...ænkel's foot ...jured. He ...annot pull his ...edge		Inventory of provisions. Food shortage. By rationing they hope to make their stores last for 3 more weeks	If they cannot shoot a seal or polar bear within three weeks (which is certainly a possibility) they will starve to death. They now realise that they will not reach land before winter and they have no choice but to attempt a wintering on the ice floe
...rindberg's foot ...out of sorts		No entries from Andrée or Strindberg	
...ænkel's foot ...jured. No ...ention of ...rindberg's foot, ...t it may be ...sumed that it ...d not get well ...tween the 14th ...d 16th Sep			They are concerned about the food situation – it has been weeks since they shot a polar bear
...ænkel's foot ...ured		Andrée shoots a seal, probably a ringed seal (no. 1). They reckon it will feed them for three weeks	They are eating both seal intestines (which can lead to botulism) and seal liver (which can cause hypervitaminosis A)
		Andrée: *All parts of the seal taste good fried. The meat in particular and the blubber go down well*	
...ænkel's foot still ...ured		Strindberg: *We have decided to stay on the ice floe**	*Andrée apparently came to this decision, according to his diary, as early as 12-13th Sep

Date	Weather	Food consumption	Physical activity	Mental state
17 Sep 1897	Temperature -3° Wind NW 5.2 m/s Effective temperature -9° Precipitation 10 Light snowfall White Island sighted	The following parts of the seal are consumed: Brain, intestines, liver, lungs, meat, blubber, kidneys, heart, stomach, stomach contents, blood	They stay put on the ice floe	Andrée: *It is worrying that we have not seen any game to shoot. Our stores must be supplemented soon and richly if we are to have any chance of enduring. [...] The mood is fairly good, though jokes and smiles are rare. [...] My young companions are holding up better than I had dared to hope. The fact that we have been drifting rapidly south for the last few days is likely in some measure responsible for our confidence*
18 Sep 1897	Temperature -3° Wind NW 2.1 m/s Effective temperature -6° Precipitation 10	Banquet: Seal steak and ivory gull fried in butter and seal blubber, seal liver, seal brain and seal kidney. Butter and Schumacher bread. Wine. Lactoserin cocoa with Mellin's food, Albert biscuits and butter, Stauffer raisin gateau with raspberry syrup. Port wine 1834 Antonio de Ferrara gifted by the King. Boström cheese with butter and crackers. A glass of wine	They stay put on the ice floe	Andrée: *The mood was outstanding and we went to bed full and content* Strindberg: *Festivities*
19 Sept 1897	Temperature -5° Wind SE 0.8 m/s Effective temperature -5°	Frænkel cooks a delicious blood pancake using 0.6 lbs seal blood, 0.3 lbs finely chopped seal meat, 0.4 oz flour, a knife's edge of salt and one of dry yeast. Andrée: *At last the pancake fails to inspire the revulsion that at least S. and I felt during a couple of times during the first few days we relied on seal meat and blubber*	They stay put on the ice floe. Strindberg begins construction on a snow shelter	In good spirits. They now reckon their provisions will last until the end of February. Andrée: *Yesterday seems to have been the first in a lucky series of fortunate days. One now considers one's prospects with considerably elevated expectations**

...mptoms/injuries	Medication	Miscellaneous	Comments
...ndrée: *Frænkel's* ...ot still injured ...d will likely ...main so for 1 to ...weeks ...rindberg's feet ...oth injured ·		They spot land! They have no plans of making landfall on White Island, however; it seems impossible since the island is covered by a large glacier. Andrée calls the island, which has not yet been put on the map, New Iceland Andrée: *We spotted a bear on land. [...] The distance to the glacier is estimated to be 6 miles*	There are polar bears on White Island
		25th anniversary of Oscar II's ascent to the throne Andrée shoots a seal (no. 2) The ice floe they are on drifts past White Island, along its east side. The island (which Andrée calls New Iceland and the others call White Island) remains in view all day	They have hauled both wine and port all this way! Shouldn't the wine be frozen solid by now?
		Andrée shoots 2 seals (no. 3 and 4) and 1 bearded seal (no. 1) Frænkel shoots an ivory gull, Strindberg kills 4 ivory gulls with one shot, *our favourite diversion!* Andrée has now taken to calling the island White Island as well	*So they have previously had low expectations with regards to their prospects They are still in no hurry to construct their shelter. Strindberg calls the room where they are to sleep *the roaster*. Clearly they are not cold inside the hut

Date	Weather	Food consumption	Physical activity	Mental state
20 Sep 1897	Temperature -3.5° Wind SE 3.6 m/s Effective temperature -8°	Soup (0.8 lbs seal meat, 0.3 lbs seal blubber, 1.8 oz Mellin's food, the rest water). Blubber oil on Schumacher bread. Semi-cooked polar bear steak. Blood pancake (0.6 lbs polar bear blood, 0.4 lbs kidney fat from polar bear, 0.4 oz flour, salt and dry yeast, 1 knife's edge respectively). Coffee

Their stove is working fitfully.

Andrée: *It is a grave misfortune that the spare parts for this were left in Pike's house!* (on Danes Island) | They stay put on the ice floe. Strindberg works on the snow shelter | Andrée: ... *even though we have not been able to avoid the occurrence of mutual antagonism. I do hope, however, that this seed shall not take root and grow** |
21 Sep 1897	Temperature -2.8° Wind NE 4.5 m/s Effective temperature -8°	Blood pancake of frozen seal blood. 0.6 lbs mixed with knife's edges dry yeast and salt, 3 tablespoons saltwater, 0.4 lbs chopped meat and 0.3 lbs seal blubber. It was edible after only 8 minutes but was left to fry for much longer. (*Delicious*, according to Andrée)	They stay put on the ice floe. Strindberg and Frænkel work on the snow shelter	
22 Sep 1897	Temperature -2° Wind NE 2.6 m/s Effective temperature -6° Precipitation 10* Visibility Heavy fog		They stay put on the ice flow. They work on the snow shelter	Suddenly they think they can hear the floe breaking (which was not the case). Andrée: ... *Square beneath the shelter, as it seemed to us. We feared we had run aground*
23 Sep 1897	Temperature -4.2° Wind E 0.7 m/s Effective temperature -4.2° Precipitation 0.4 inches	They eat the meat of the bearded seal (*tastes delicious*) Andrée: *One of the best improvements to our cooking is the addition of blood to the jus. It makes it thick and simulates the presence of bread. We have extracted every last edible part of polar bear, bearded seal, seal and ivory gull. (Bear liver excepted, obviously)**	They stay put on the ice floe. All three are now at work on the snow shelter	Andrée: ...*I believe we now have meat and fat to last well into spring. Still we must shoot more to increase our rations and secure more fuel and ligh*

mptoms/injuries	Medication	Miscellaneous	Comments
		Frænkel shoots a polar bear (no. 12). A bird is shot, probably of the species Burgomaster. They now reckon their stores will last through March. Frænkel constructs a blubber oil lamp that functions poorly Andrée: *We now have such quantities of meat, blubber etc. that it has become a challenge to protect it adequately from nocturnal bear visits. [...] The matter of finishing the house is a burning one in this cold*	*They are arguing now, despite having felt so confident about the future only yesterday Andrée mentions that the polar bear afforded them a *sizable pelt*. What are they planning to do with it? Do they mean to sleep on the fells of the polar bears they kill?
eryone is tired		Strindberg: *Bear**	*He is probably referring to the polar bear they shot on the 20th Sep Frænkel has joined the work on the shelter, are they afraid of nocturnal polar bear attacks?
		Strindberg shoots a seal (no. 5). They also shoot a couple of ivory gulls	
		Andrée: *We should be able to move our stores inside the day after tomorrow. It is much needed.* (He is referring to the need to move the meat into the shelter as quickly as possible because it is attracting polar bears)	*They are aware that polar bear liver is poisonous, but are seemingly oblivious to the fact that seal liver is too. They first eat the liver of a bearded seal sometime between the 19th and 23rd Sep They are now concerned that polar bears may come at night

Date	Weather	Food consumption	Physical activity	Mental state
24 Sept 1897	Temperature -1.8° Wind N 3.3 m/s Effective temperature -6° Precipitation 10* Visibility Heavy fog		They stay put on the ice floe. They work on the snow shelter	
25 Sept 1897	Temperature -1.8° Wind N 8 m/s Effective temperature -9° Precipitation 10*		They stay put on the ice floe. They work on the snow shelter	
26 Sept 1897	Temperature -0.5° Wind N 5.5 m/s Effective temperature -6°		They stay put on the ice floe. They work on the snow shelter	
27 Sept 1897	Temperature -2° Wind N 5.0 m/s Effective temperature -7° Precipitation Rain		They stay put on the ice floe. They work on the snow shelter	
28 Sept 1897	Temperature -2.2° Wind N 3.9 m/s Effective temperature -7°		They work on the snow shelter and move in, even though it is not quite finished	
29 Sept 1897	Temperature -1.2° Wind S 3.3 m/s Effective temperature -5°	Polar bear	They stay put on the ice floe. They work on the snow shelter	Andrée: *On the other hand the bears come flocking. [...] We have been forced to store the meat inside to protect ourselves from bears*

mptoms/injuries	Medication	Miscellaneous	Comments
		Polar bear in the camp during the night. Andrée: *The bear tries to drag the bearded seal off twice [...] which we would have lost had not S. managed to get so close to the bear that it was scared off*	Strindberg is not afraid of approaching the polar bear in an attempt to run it off
		Polar bear in the camp during the night The expedition has now drifted south of Kvitøya and is taken west by the currents, around the island's southern point	
eryone is tired		All three men shoot one (the same) polar bear. A large, old male (no. 13) The bearded seal is still in the camp Andrée has reverted to calling the island New Iceland Andrée: *Our ice floe is diminishing at a worrying rate in the vicinity of our shelter*	Their relocation into the half-finished shelter is motivated by a fear of polar bears They move the meat into the shelter to protect themselves, not the meat

Date	Weather	Food consumption	Physical activity	Mental state
30 Sept 1897	Temperature -7.1° Wind N 2.1 m/s Effective temperature -11° Visibility Stratocumulus	Polar bear	They stay put on the ice floe. They work on the snow shelter	
1 Oct 1897	Temperature -4.4° Later -10 Wind 2.3 m/s Effective temperature -8° — -15° Precipitation 10	Polar bear	They stay put on the ice floe. They work on the snow shelter and hope to finish it by the 2nd Oct	Andrée: *A good day. The evening was as spectacularly beautiful as any man could wish*
2 Oct 1897	Temperature -9° Visibility Clear, sunshine	Polar bear	They stay put on the ice floe	Suddenly the ice floe breaks apart and is flooded. Andrée: *Our position and prospects were radically altered. The shelter and the ice floe were no protection and yet we had to remain there, for the present at least. [...] We could resume working without delay.* No one had lost their determination*
3 Oct 1897	Temperature -6.2° Wind N 0.9 m/s Effective temperature -6.2° Precipitation Stratocumulus Alto... Frænkel's last entry		On the ice floe. They work to gather up provisions and gear	Strindberg: *Interesting situation**
4 Oct 1897			On the ice floe. Flensing of downed game	*Interesting situation*

5 OCTOBER: THE EXPEDITION REACHES THE SHORES OF WHITE ISLAND

ymptoms/injuries	Medication	Miscellaneous	Comments
		All gear, meat and other provisions are spread across several ice floes	The shelter, the result of two weeks of labour, has been destroyed. They are, once more, unprotected against polar bears *They must not be too physically weakened since they can resume work without delay
			This entry is scrawled across both the 3rd and 4th Oct and indicates, according to 19th century usage, an unpleasant, taxing situation
		They start considering whether it might be possible to make landfall on what they call the *lowland*, a small beach at the southern point of White Island	The last day on the ice

WIND CHILL. TEMPERATURE ADJUSTED FOR WIND SPEED.
When it is windy, it feels colder than the temperature indicated by a
thermometer. I adjust Frænkel's temperature notations from his meteorological journal.

	Wind speed					
Recorded temp	0 m/s	5 m/s	10 m/s	15 m/s	20 m/s	25 m/s
-0°C	-0°C	-5°C	-7°C	-8°C	-9°C	-10°C
-2°C	-2°C	-7°C	-10°C	-11°C	-12°C	-13°C
-4°C	-4°C	-10°C	-12°C	-14°C	-15°C	-16°C
-6°C	-6°C	-12°C	-15°C	-17°C	-18°C	-19°C
-8°C	-8°C	-15°C	-18°C	-19°C	-21°C	-22°C
-10°C	-10°C	-17°C	-20°C	-22°C	-23°C	-25°C
-12°C	-12°C	-20°C	-23°C	-25°C	-26°C	-27°C
-14°C	-14°C	-22°C	-26°C	-28°C	-29°C	-30°C
-16°C	-16°C	-25°C	-28°C	-30°C	-32°C	-33°C
-18°C	-18°C	-27°C	-31°C	-33°C	-35°C	-36°C
-20°C	-20°C	-30°C	-34°C	-36°C	-38°C	-39°C
-22°C	-22°C	-32°C	-36°C	-39°C	-40°C	-42°C
-24°C	-24°C	-35°C	-39°C	-41°C	-43°C	-45°C
-26°C	-26°C	-37°C	-41°C	-44°C	-46°C	-48°C
-28°C	-28°C	-40°C	-44°C	-47°C	-49°C	-50°C
-30°C	-30°C	-42°C	-47°C	-50°C	-52°C	-53°C

WHAT THE DIARIES ACTUALLY TELL US: Andrée, Strindberg and Frænkel slipped into meltwater ponds and water-filled fissures in the ice again and again, which *chilled* them. Their *feet were wet* because they trudged through ice sludge. Their packing baskets were soaked, and a sledge with wet stores is much heavier than a dry one. They were so exhausted they felt obliged to reiterate it constantly in their diaries; *severe exhaustion* is mentioned nine times. All three suffered from *colds*, described as "permanent catarrh" in early August. Several weeks later Andrée made renewed mention of his cold.

They suffered digestive problems repeatedly. They took both morphine and opium to relieve *stomach pains* and *diarrhoea*. That Andrée had severe diarrhoea is stated five times in the diaries. The diarrhoea alternated with *constipation*, which is mentioned four times. Frænkel seems to have come down with diarrhoea at an early stage of their march across the sea ice; it is mentioned four times in August. He also endured recurring abdominal pain. On the 9th September the diaries inform us that he had been complaining of stomach ache more or less non-stop. Strindberg had diarrhoea too, as mentioned in mid-August. All three men were afflicted with digestive distress, but that is not necessarily indicative of a fatal underlying disease. They ate raw entrails and poorly cooked polar bear and seal meat, which would have been crawling with enough bacteria to make anyone ill. They took opium and morphine for the pain and the diarrhoea, which, in turn, led to constipation.

Frænkel seems to have been worst affected. He pulled the heaviest load; the boat, packed full of supplies, was lashed to the top of his sledge. When they set off, he was hauling 460 pounds. Before the journey was undertaken, Frænkel had been presented as the physically superior member of the group: in his application to join the expedition he wrote that he *possesses a healthy and strong physique and is used to hard work and hiking through difficult terrain.* He failed to mention the surgery he had undergone five years previous for sciatica, which had forced him to give up plans for a military career. Aside from being weakened by digestive illness, his feet also began giving him trouble, making it difficult for him to haul his own sledge. Andrée wrote about Frænkel's *foot injury* (left foot) for the first time in mid-August. He did not mention the cause of the injury, but at first it could be alleviated with massage. Eventually, the state of Frænkel's foot deteriorated to the point where he could no longer pull his own sledge at all. His foot injury seems to have had a profound effect on the expedition since the diaries mention it ten times.

Frænkel starts experiencing *spasms*, probably in the muscles of his legs, in August; on one occasion, when Andrée was holding his legs down, Frænkel jerked so violently his "knee was pulled out of joint". (It is not possible to dislocate one's own knee. It is, however, possible to twist it and thus dislocate the knee cap.) On the 9th August, less than a month into their march, Andrée wrote about Frænkel that *little appears to remain of his moral strength*. In the context of nineteenth century discourse, which was habitually less than candid, and of a diary that was consciously composed with an eye to posterity, this was a euphemism for Frænkel falling apart. In September, an *abscess* on Frænkel's foot, probably the left one, is mentioned. In one diary entry, Frænkel is said to experience eye symptoms, which could be interpreted as *snow blindness*.

Strindberg developed foot complaints too. A *sore toe* is mentioned in mid-August. Was it blisters? Boots that pinched? Two days later, Strindberg was afflicted with *spasms*. It is not clear in what part of the body. A *foot injury* was noted for the first time at the end of August. Several weeks later the injury is mentioned again. A few days later, both of Strindberg's feet hurt, as mentioned twice in the diaries. He developed an *abscess* on his upper lip and *cut* his hand. Both Strindberg and Frænkel had sore feet, but that is not necessarily indicative of an underlying disease that would eventually claim their lives on White Island. Sprains and blisters are common on polar expeditions.

There are no mentions of frostbite, unless that was the cause of the blisters. Andrée only states that they felt cold three times. At no point in the diaries is it said that anyone had a fever.

They make landfall on White Island on the 5th October. All diary entries cease on the 8th October. The final four pages, written on White Island, are difficult to make out. The pages have disintegrated and only fragments of some of the words remain.

5 OCTOBER

the 5th in the morni
the previously mentio
we had   *of the island*
luckily we
there and one
ing the
I *assisted*
Greew. t me
along the glacier
from the glac*ier*
not our hard
than late at night
the day's frantic work
in the middle of the night and
            to the *south*
because beyond the *cove*
the northern lights neither *lig*
warmed. The cooking stove
ac   g u   in and to
  il   y   i
did not get   bed un
til
– my *m   r*th*day*
We ~~and~~ hereby c   tly
christened the region around
site "M*i*   Land"

roman font: legible text.
italics: possibly legible text.

Entry in Strindberg's almanac: *Moved ashore.*

They hauled three heavy sledges, a boat and large quantities of seal and polar bear meat across the pack ice to the island. We don't know where on the beach they pitched their tent.

They must not have been too weakened physically, since they were able to complete the *day's frantic work.*

Something must have happened to the *cooking stove* that day, or Andrée would not have mentioned it in his diary. Were they forced to eat the meat raw?

The course of events on White Island is open to different interpretations, depending on how the gaps are filled.

Pallin's interpretation (author of *The Andrée Mystery*), 1934.	Reverend Helgesson's somewhat less cheery interpretation in *Svenska Dagbladet*, 1931.
The cooking stove was once again **acting up** and failing, **and to** boil or fry on it was impossible. We **did not get** to **bed** un-til the morning of the following day	**The cooking stove** was irrevocably lost **in** the dark and we could not find it again. everything was darkness and toil – making notes in the dark of midnight about the day which
– **my m**other's b**irthday** **We and hereby c**onsequently **christened the region** around this new	– **my m**ost abject **day** **We and hereby c**onsequently **christened the region** around our new camping
site **"Mi**na Andrée's **Land"**	site the **"Mo**onless **Land"**

Mina Andrée was Andrée's mother. She passed away the spring before the expedition set off. Her birthday was the 6th October.

6 OCTOBER

during the day the 6th
strong winds t
were not much able
yet under*took* a short
eventually we
. Swedes
to be the
i   icy
which soon interes-
t we found ~~there~~ high
above the sea
. the ground all
ffs – *gran* – crushed rock
some of the gravel was
The gravel was ~~lay~~ partly
spread out   *by* great ridges
me   which were however
vered so that it was not possible
along   the whole
ly   *the land* strongly
ing   *times*
ning   in the dark
b   *t* of the snow-
hut   ransporting of the goods
to its   vicinity. This was
heavy   so *n*   mpleted.

From Strindberg's almanac: *Blizzard reconnaissance* (Stubbendorf at first took this nearly illegible word to read *resignation*).

Did they spend this day by the tent on account of the blizzard? They do some reconnaissance. Andrée writes that the ground is covered in **crushed rock** and **gravel**, so it must not be entirely snow covered at this point.

They do something **in the dark** – do they start the building of a snow hut? Does **heavy** indicate heavy work, as in pulling the sledges over to their new campsite?

I was about to
feared that
such a *one*
we have s*e*
thereby
ments *f*
cier, *which* g
had stepped onto
if it might possibly
to look at *tr*   *t*
the glacier *wa*
must ~~surely~~ *be taller*
than one at *first in* ~~sto~~ *imagines*
a bear could be seen *pe p*
the sea but k *he avoi*   *u*
not heard from since. Foxes *h*
seen. The *worst predators*
lls *t*
our camp   *meat*
and that   *sickening*
and internal *ivalry and* envy
now make the impressio   innocent white doves without   scavenging
birds.

7 OCTOBER

Strindberg's almanac: *Relocation*. Andree's diary indicates that they moved the sledges to a new tent site on the 6th October. Who got the date wrong?

They pitched their tent at the new campsite. They spotted a polar **bear** out on the sea ice. **The worst predators** here are the ivory gulls that circle **our camp** and the **meat** store? It would seem, then, that they have lugged the meat stores over to the new campsite.

Pallin's interpretation	Helgesson's interpretation
I was about to start moving the hut because I	**I was about to** lose my courage and
feared that it might, by a snowstorm, should	**feared that** we would be turned over by
such a one hit, and	**such a** strong wind. But
we have seen our share since yesterday,	**we have s**uffered neither cold nor injury
thereby be snowed under and not meet our require-	**thereby.**
ments for winter quarters.	

8 OCTOBER

dreadful weather and we fea-
remain in the tent all day.
wood to
he hut
not to be obliged,
– unlike
on the sea
crashing, creaking
ale and driftwood
s move *around* a little
ermits.

Pallin's interpretation	Helgesson's interpretation
On 8th we had **dreadful weather and we fea-** red we would have to **remain in the tent all day.**	Still **dreadful weather and we fea-** red we would have to **remain in the tent all day.**
We did, however, fetch **wood to** use as beams for **the hut**'s roof. It feels good **not to be obliged,** here on dry land – **unlike** before on the pack ice **on the sea**	We collected drift**wood to** be able to start laying the roof of **the hut.** We did this so as **not to be obliged** to curve it – **unlike** with the hut out **on the sea** From out there we hear constant
constantly to hear **crashing, creaking** and rumbling. Bones from wh**ale and driftwood** we can collect and thus **move around a little**	**crashing, creaking** and rumbling. We collect whalebones **and driftwood** at times. That lets us **move around a little**
when the weather **permits.**	whenever the weather **permits.**

They seem to have been planning to build a **hut**. Is that what they are collecting whalebones **and driftwood** for? Both whale ribs and driftwood were found in the camp when it was discovered.

The very last sentence Andrée wrote seems to suggest that they were neither sick nor weakened; they seem to have longed to get out of the tent, to **move around a little**.

This is where Andrée's diary ends. Ever since take-off from Danes Island, three months previous, he had written daily entries. After their arrival on White Island, he conscientiously wrote a full page every day, but on the 8th October he stopped half way down a page. Then the entries stop.

My   .   we awoke around 12 o'cl. but
since it was raining and   we dozed in the
tent until 3. Then we rose and I cooked a spot
of food (lactoserin cocoa with condensed milk
and biscuits and sandwiches). At 4.30 o'cl.
we set off and have now trudged and hauled
our heavy sledges for 4½ hours. The weather
is fairly dreadful: wet snow and fog. But we are
in good humour. We have kept up a really very
pleasant conversation all day long, Andrée has
told us of his life how, he came to work at the
patent office etc. Frænkel and Andrée have
gone on ahead to reconnoitre and I stayed
with the sledges and am now sitting here
writing to you.

Well, now it is evening where you are and I hope your day has been thoroughly merry and pleasant. Here each day is like the one before. Pull and haul the sledges eat and sleep. The happiest hou   of each day is when I lie down to rest and allow my thoughts to drift to better and happier times, but our immediate goal is now our wintering location where we hope to be in a better position. Now the others are returning and we shall resume our toil with the sledges. Au revoir.

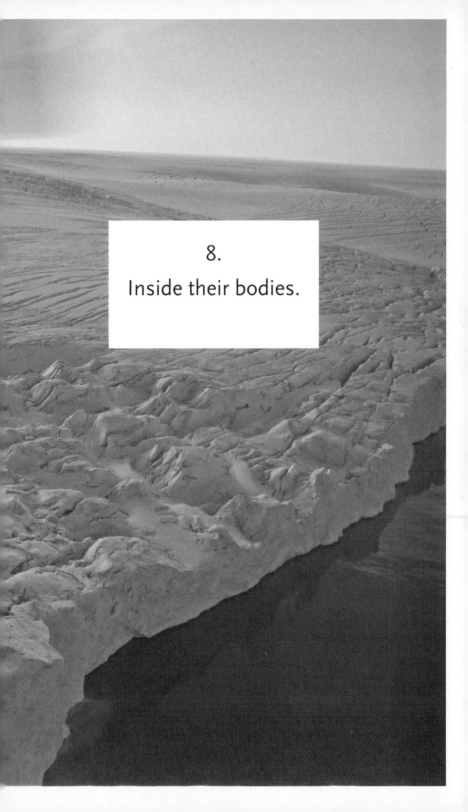

8.
Inside their bodies.

I HAVE COME HERE SO MANY TIMES. The shelves lining the walls of the Andrée Museum's basement are filled with drab archive boxes made of acid free cardboard. I read and read, without really knowing what I am looking for. I flip through thousands of pages. Many pounds' worth of correspondence. Loan contracts. French receipts from 1895 for the purchase of balloon cloth, several copies on purple paper. Detailed letters to near and dear ones written in pencil in the florid, even hand of Nils Strindberg. I get dizzy trying to decipher the nineteenth century handwriting. Hidden among school diplomas, banquet menus and vaccination cards are fourteen flimsy, typed A3 pages. I could easily have flipped past them. When real evidence and meaningless junk are intermingled, everything seems equally important. I read the header. I read it again. This is an autopsy report. An autopsy report regarding the Andrée expedition. None of the researchers trying to establish the cause of their death has ever mentioned an autopsy report. I have never read anything about an autopsy report in any of the books. Has no one seen these documents before? *Report on the investigation of the human remains of the members of S.A. Andrée's polar expedition,* signed Gunnar Hedrén, professor of forensic medicine and pathology at Karolinska Institutet, Stockholm's medical university, 1930.

When M/S Braatvaag returned from White Island, it headed for Tromsø. The boxes containing the human remains were brought ashore and transported to the basement of the city's only hospital, where a small group of Norwegian and Swedish doctors were waiting. The autopsy was begun that same day. The tattered garments were carefully unwrapped, layer by layer, revealing tissue and skeletal parts. The condition of the clothing was documented: whether buttons were done up or not. Whether socks were held in place by puttees. Every splinter, indentation and material loss of the bones was recorded. Two days of measuring and matching later, the doctors concluded that the bodies found on White Island belonged to Andrée and Strindberg. Nils' younger brother, Tore Strindberg, had travelled up from Stockholm and participated in the cataloguing of Nils Strindberg's remains. A chipped front tooth helped him identify his brother's cranium. The doctors inferred that Frænkel never made it to White Island, that he must have drowned out on the ice. Two weeks after the completion of the autopsy, Stubbendorff's ship sailed into Tromsø harbour with more crates from White Island. One more autopsy was conducted in the basement of Kysthospitalet; this time the remains discovered seemed to be Frænkel's. In addition, Andrée's cranium, spine, pelvis and left femur could be identified.

WHAT I GATHER FROM THE AUTOPSY REPORT:

[×] The skeletal parts show no signs of crush injuries. No bones are broken.
[×] The skeletal parts show signs of minor damage, such as chipping. Many parts of their skeletons are missing entirely, no big surprise, given that polar bears would have had access to them.
[×] There is nothing to indicate bone thickening or tooth loss, which would be the classic signs of scurvy.
[×] Frænkel wore neither shoes nor mittens when he died.
[×] Andrée had Strindberg's personal effects in his jacket pocket.
[×] For some reason, Andrée and Frænkel's craniums were sawn in half during the autopsy, to investigate the contents. Strindberg's cranium was left entire.
[×] The bodies had lain unprotected for three decades and should have been stripped clean of flesh within a year or two. But muscle tissue was still attached to almost every skeletal part, indicating that the bodies had, for the most part, been covered by ice and snow. Large patches of skin and hair were still attached to

Frænkel's cranium. Strindberg's clothes were so full of remains they had to be rinsed at least ten times before they were fit to be laundered. When his long johns were rinsed, a pendant with three charms, a heart, a cross and an anchor, was discovered.

[x] Suddenly, there is a sentence that stops me dead. There was a round hole the size of a penny in Strindberg's forehead. *Did Andrée and Frænkel shoot Strindberg?!* In 1930, a Swedish penny had a diameter of .6 inches. But the calibre of the expedition's ammunition was too small (.13 cal, .28 cal and .45 cal) to have made the hole. Moreover, the word used in the report, *defect*, suggests that this was an indentation rather than a hole penetrating the skull. The damage might have been caused by a polar bear's claws or teeth, but that is largely irrelevant since Strindberg's cranium was not buried under rocks like the rest of his body, and thus protected. The cranium was found on the ground, outside the grave. The damage to his forehead could just as easily have been caused after his death.

[x] Nowhere does the autopsy report mention tissue samples from the remains. Such samples are normally collected if the cause of death is unknown. The purpose of the autopsy seems rather to have been to put the right bones in the right coffin. Had there been just a small sample from the bodies to analyse, I could have tested for lethal levels of, for example, lead, morphine and opium. But no samples were collected during the autopsy.

ANDRÉE'S REMAINS ON WHITE ISLAND

As recorded in the autopsy report

1. The cranium, complete with mandible, was found separated from the body, some distance removed from the tent. The right temporal bone and parts of the right parietal bone and frontal bone were damaged when the cranium was hacked out of the ice. The skull was otherwise unharmed. A partly decomposed lump of brain tissue, the size of a fist, was found inside the cranium.

2. A considerable amount of severely decomposed muscle tissue was still attached to the left side of the face. The maxilla contained 11 strong teeth. The mandible contained 14 strong teeth. All teeth were unharmed, but noticeably worn down.

3. Half of the right clavicle and rib fragments were discovered separately. It was not firmly established that these belonged to Andrée. Minor rib fragments were found among the tattered clothing on the ledge where Andrée's lower body was discovered. His right arm and hand were missing.

4. The left humerus was discovered among the tattered clothing on the ledge where Andrée's lower body was found. The bone was undamaged and completely skeletonised. The lower part of the bone was wrapped in parts of a sleeve, consisting of a coarse sweater, a knitted blue and white striped jumper and, innermost, a linen shirt.

5. Several vertebrae, the pelvis and the left femur were found near the tent. Vertebrae C1–3 were missing. Vertebrae C4–5 (as well as some rib fragments attached to their respective vertebrae), the pelvis and the left femur constituted an intact anatomical unit. Several of the vertebrae showed signs of minor, superficial damage to the anterior segments. The vertebrae were otherwise well preserved.

6. The pelvis (including the sacrum) was connected to the spine. The iliac crest of pelvis was severely damaged as were the adjacent sections of the hip bone. The lower quarter of the sacrum was missing a break was indicated by the exposed cancellous surface (inner, porous skeletal tissue). Small amounts of severely decomposed, unidentifiable tissue were found in the synovial cavity of each hip bone.

7. The left radius and ulna were found further from the tent. The ulna showed signs of very minor damage at the lower end, toward the hand. The left hand was not found.

8. The right femur was discovered further from the tent. It was 20 inches long and damaged at the neck.

9. The left femur was 20 inches long and connected to the synovial joint of the left hip bone. The femur was completely skeletonised and undamaged. The articular capsule between the pelvis and the femur was preserved.

10. The right lower leg and foot were found wearing long johns, trousers and leather boots, on a ledge above the tent. The tibia and fibula lay side by side. They were not organically connected. The upper end of the fibula showed minor damage below the head. Some traces of tendons were attached to the superior end of the tibia.

11. The lower left leg and foot were found wearing long johns, trousers and leather boots, on a ledge above the tent. The

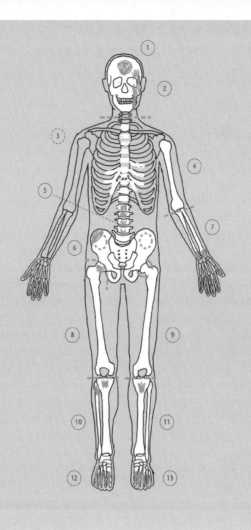

tibia and fibula lay side by side. They were not organically joined. Parts of the patellar ligament were still present on the tibia.

2. The right foot had been completely detached from the lower leg. The plantar fascia, the fascia of the sole of the foot, was so well preserved it still held the adjacent foot bones together. All the bones of the foot were found. Decomposed muscle tissue was attached to several individual foot bones and tendons. A section of the

Achilles' tendon was still attached to the calcaneus.

13. The left foot had been completely detached from the lower leg. All the bones of the foot were found. Decomposed muscle tissue was attached to several individual foot bones and tendons. A section of the Achilles' tendon was still attached to the calcaneus.

STRINDBERG'S REMAINS ON WHITE ISLAND

As recorded in the autopsy report

1. Strindberg's body was found buried under rocks in a crevice, 92 feet from the tent. The cranium and mandible were discovered outside the grave, 7–10 feet from the body. The cervical vertebrae were not connected. One superior vertebra was missing.

2. Both collar bones were found loose inside the ribcage. The left scapula was found on top of the grave. The organs of the throat and chest were missing. The right scapula was in the anatomical position.

3. Some of the superior ribs had been dislodged from their vertebrae. Several ribs were organically connected to their vertebrae. There was no costal cartilage. Some minor remnants of the intercostal muscles and the pleura were recorded, forming a blackish brown slush on the inside of the collapsed ribcage. The parts of the sternum lay on top of the thoracic vertebrae.

4. The right humerus was found in the anatomical position along the side of the ribcage.

5. The left humerus rested along the left side of the ribcage. It was not organically connected to the rest of the skeleton.

6. The superior thoracic vertebrae were disconnected. One superior thoracic vertebra was missing. All other thoracic and lumbar vertebrae formed a connected portion of the spine.

7. The right radius and ulna were found in the anatomical position along the side of the ribcage.

8. The pelvis, including the sacrum, was not connected to the rest of the skeleton. A lump of blackish grey slush the size of a child's head, consisting of decomposed organs and intestines was found in the lesser pelvis. Some curly, dark brown hairs were found on either side of the pubic bone. During the undressing, decomposed muscle stuck to the inside of the inmost pair of underwear.

9. The abdominal area was depressed lengthwise, causing the space between the lower ribs and the pelvis to be significantly compressed. A large section of the left half of the diaphragm was still intact.

10. The left radius and ulna were positioned adjacent to the left side of the lower edge of the ribcage, side by side. There was no organic connection. Just below the bones of the forearm were a handful of carpal bones and among these bones, which were jumbled, a gold ring was found, marked Anna Charlier. The metacarpals and fingers were missing.

11. The right hand was positioned centrally on the chest, by the costal margin. The second, third and fourth metacarpals as well as the intact second, third and fourth fingers were found. The metacarpals were organically connected to each other and to their respective fingers. The nail of the index finger was still attached. The bones of the fingers were connected by tissue, sticky, soft and discoloured but structurally intact. The thumb, complete with nail, lay loose next to the hand, together with a fifth metacarpal and a collection of carpal bones.

12. The right femur was completely skeletonised and had no organic connection to the rest of the skeleton.

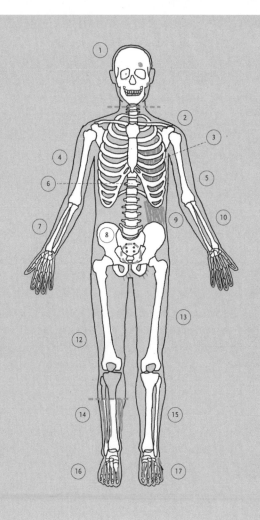

. The left femur was completely skeletonised and had no organic connection to the rest of the skeleton.

. The lower right leg had been broken some way below the knee when the body was excavated – the upper thirds of the tibia and fibula were missing. The tibia and the fibula were enveloped in severely decomposed muscle tissue.

. The left tibia and fibula were not organically connected.

16. The right foot was not connected to the lower leg. The individual bones of the foot had come apart. Small amounts of decomposed muscle and ligaments were attached to these bones.

17. The left foot was not attached to the lower leg. The individual bones of the foot had for the most part come apart. Small amounts of decomposed muscle and ligaments were attached to these bones.

STRINDBERG'S CRANIUM ON WHITE ISLAND
As recorded in the autopsy report

The cranium and mandible were found on the ground, 7–10 feet from Strindberg's grave. The mandible was detached from the cranium. The horizontal circumference of the cranium was 22 inches. Unlike the reports on Andrée and Frænkel's craniums, no mention is made of residual brain tissue. The cranium was intact except for the damages outlined below:

1. An indentation the size of a penny in the anterior wall of the left side of the frontal bone. (The diameter of a Swedish penny in 1930: 0.6 inches.)
2. Insignificant damage on the floor of the right eye socket.
3. Minor damage on the rim of the right eye socket and on the adjacent part of the maxilla.
4. Some small damage, approximately .5 inches across, on the left zygomatic process.
5. No teeth were missing from the maxilla apart from the hindmost molar on the right side. The right central incisor was chipped. The central and right lateral mandibular incisors were missing. Other than that the teeth of the lower jaw were intact. All teeth were healthy and distinctly white. Some of the premolars and molars in both the upper and lower jaw had occlusal fillings.

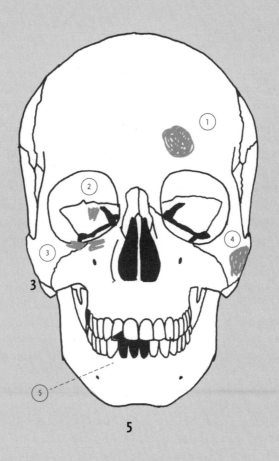

3

5

1. The upper half of Frænkel's body was found by the tent, lying on its left side, his head resting on his left arm. The cranium, thoracic vertebrae, left arm and left hand were all connected. The cranium was virtually undamaged. The largest horizontal circumference was 21 inches. A lump of decomposed tissue the size of an orange was found inside the skull.

2. There were 15 healthy teeth in the maxilla. There were 13 teeth in the mandible. All teeth were intact and showed no significant signs of wear. The projections of the right-hand processes of the mandible were missing; rough surfaces indicate a break.

3. Two ribs were packed in a separate parcel. The parcel also contained pieces of scalp, two the size of a palm, the rest smaller. Some of the pieces had a scattering of light brown hairs loosely attached. It would appear the scalp was separated from the cranium when it was excavated.

4. The right humerus was found separately at the periphery of the camp. The bone was wrapped in a striped linen sleeve.

5. The left humerus was not connected to the bones of the forearm. The inferior half of the humerus was sheathed in a significant amount of decomposed muscle.

6. Ten loose vertebrae were found inside Frænkel's clothing. Seven rib fragments were also discovered, of which two were still attached to their respective vertebra, as well as one scapula and one collar bone. Decomposing muscle, fatty tissue and dermis were present on the posterior side of one vertebra.

7. The left radius and ulna were organically connected and covered in significant amounts of decomposing muscle.

8. The right radius, ulna and hand were not found.

9. The pelvis (including the sacrum) and four connected lumbar vertebrae (L2–5) were found 165 feet from the camp. A piece of L2, constituting approximately a third of the body of the vertebra, was attached to L3. L3–L5 showed signs of minor anterior bone density reduction. They were connected by ligaments. A few areas showing signs of decreased bone density, characterised by cancellous (internal, porous) bone tissue, were noted on the superior anterior edge of the pubic bone. The iliac crest on the left hip bone showed signs of gnawing, particularly on the inside of the pelvis, leaving mostly the cortical substance of the outer surface of the iliac crest (external, harder bone tissue). The surface of the exposed trabecular bone (internal, porous bone tissue) was uneven and jagged.

10. The left hand was connected to the bones of the forearm by tendons and decomposed tissue. The bones of the hand, all of which were found, were covered in decomposing tissue. The nail of some fingers were still attached.

11. The right femur, tibia, fibula and foot were found still connected on the outskirts of the campsite. The head of the femur was missing. Its condyles were connected to the bones of the lower leg by intact intra and extracapsular ligaments.

12. The left leg and foot were not found.

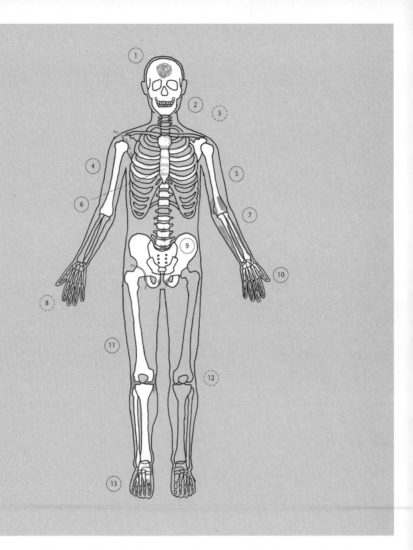

3. All five metatarsal bones of the right foot were found. They were loosely connected at the posterior end by residual soft tissue. A handful of connected tarsal bones were found attached to the metatarsals. The right talus bone was found separately. There was no boot on the foot.

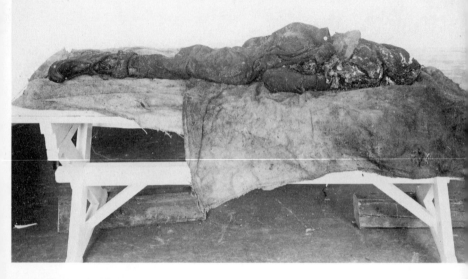

Nils Strindberg (from front)

Nils Strindberg (from behind)

Woke at 11.30am
Cooked and saw to equipment
Set out at 2.15pm

Treacherous lead, Andrée and I had a
disagreement over the crossing of the lead.
At   a meagre lunch, after lunch walked
a mile or so (1 or 2). Made camp by a large
yellow hummock (13 feet tall). I made soup on
peas biscuits stock capsules and Rosseau's
pemmican.

Slept excellently and dreamed about you Anna
an unpleasant dream. I dreamt, you see, that
I had entirely forgotten that Anna had come
to Stockholm to spend a Sunday with me and
that, you see, I had not gone to meet you. I
did not remember it until that evening and
I and ran down to Wasagatan to beg your
forgiveness. Well it was silly.

WHAT SALOMON AUGUST ANDRÉE HAD ON WHEN HE DIED

Upper body apparel	Lower body apparel
His tattered clothes were found in a bundle. Everything was covered in silvery and light yellow hairs, 2–4 inches long	Outermost: Trousers. The trousers had been worn with braces – a tab was still attached to one of the buttons
Five layers of clothing on the upper body	Thick, brown, woollen long johns
Outermost: Blue cloth jacket	Innermost: Thinner long johns
Vest	Knitted knee pads of grey wool
White sweater	Dark brown puttees with bobbles, attached to the laces of his boots
Woollen jumper with broad blue and white stripes	On his left foot: Two thin woollen socks and a calf-length knitted wool sock
Innermost: A flannel shirt	On his right foot: A thicker sock and a knitted wool sock
	Boots on his feet

Hat, mittens

Andrée was still wearing a hat when his cranium was hacked out of the ice. The hat was not brought back from White Island. Knitted mittens

Personal effects

In the inner pocket of Andrée's jacket: A pencil, a pedometer and his second diary. 4.5 pages have been used. The last entry: 8 October 1897

In the outer pockets of the jacket: Andrée's chronometer on a gold chain that had belonged to his mother. Three charms were attached to the chain: a gold ring, a heart, a locket with photographs of Andrée's parents. A tube of lanolin (for chapped or frostbitten lips and hands). A handkerchief

In another jacket pocket: A purse containing Strindberg's personal affects, among other things a locket with a photograph of Anna Charlier and a lock of her hair. A charm in the shape of a boar, which had also belonged to Strindberg. A key to one of the padlocks used to secure the private sacks of the members of the expedition, 4.25 in Swedish change and 0.55 in Norwegian coinage

In the vest: Strindberg's chronometer and a pencil stub

In his right trouser pocket: A box of matches, a pocketknife and seven cartridges usable in any of the three rifles brought on the expedition

WHAT NILS STRINDBERG HAD ON WHEN HE DIED

Upper body apparel

Four layers of clothing:

Outermost: Unbuttoned vest of thick, dark blue cloth, lined with wool (Strindberg's corpse wore no jacket)

Jumper of an unidentified type. Is only mentioned in the autopsy report, not in any of the more recent inventories

Wool shirt with breast and hems of striped linen

Innermost: An undershirt of wool

Strindberg's outer jacket was found rolled up and tied with cord at the campsite

Lower body apparel

Outermost: Dark blue cloth trousers

Thick long johns

Innermost: Thinner long johns

Thick knee-high socks knitted in a chequered pattern

Innermost: Thin woollen socks

Black puttees with bobbles

Boots filled with shoe hay

Hat, mittens

Strindberg's chequered black and white hat was found in the camp. He was not wearing mittens

Personal effects

In his left vest pocket: A pencil with rubber grip

In his long johns: A pendant with three charms: heart, cross and anchor

In 1930, Strindberg's clothes (from the upper body) were rinsed at least ten times to remove soft tissue before laundering could take place. The outermost textile layer was covered with algae. Mould grew in several places. The garments were treated with water and formalin and dried in a heated drying room

WHAT KNUT FRANKEL HAD ON WHEN HE DIED

Upper body apparel	Lower body apparel
Six layers of clothing	Brown woollen knickerbockers
Outermost: Outer jacket of brown wool, with patterned black and white wool lining. Only fragments remained of a fur collar	Innermost: Long johns
	The trousers and long johns were found on the outskirts of the camp. Both were buttoned, as though in use, and severely damaged. A comparison of the tears in the trousers and those in the long johns confirm that they were identical
Grey undershirt	
Thick, knitted Icelandic jumper	
Thick frieze outer vest with a green linen lining	
Linen jumper with broad stripes	A pair of very broken boots found at the camp site were assumed to have belonged to Frænkel. The laces of the boots were untied
Innermost: Grey linen undershirt with thin black stripes	

Hat, mittens

The first reports mention Frænkel wearing a hat. No mittens

Personal effects

In his trouser pockets: Nothing

In a vest pocket: A pocketknife with a mother-of-pearl handle, in another pocket a small pencil and a whistle, a piece from a pair of sunglasses, the remains of a tie and some loose buttons

Nils Strindberg's watch

stopped at ten minutes

past twelve.

9.
Traces.

I'm visiting the National Archive in Arninge, outside Stockholm; surrounded by elderly amateur genealogists, I work my way through nineteenth century registers of Stockholm's population. I don't know half as much about my own family. I have to stop myself when I'm talking to Nils Strindberg's living relatives; I know I sound like I'm in touch with Nils and Anna on a daily basis. I go to all the places they lived. Abandoned manors. Summer houses. I pretend I'm going to a wedding near Anna's relatives in Skåne, so they won't think it strange that a stranger would travel across half the country to interrogate them about old diary entries.

More than ten years have passed since I found that book at that party. I'm trying to follow them. I'm 113 years too late.

TEXTILE CONSERVATIONIST MAUD MARCUS looks exactly like her picture in the newspaper clippings from 1978, when she was interviewed about the sensational discovery. The only difference is that her glasses are much smaller now. I don't remember anything from back then, she insists. Then she immediately launches into the story.

"In the end I did most of the work on the Andrée items. The others at the Royal Armoury's studios probably found it all a bit revolting. We were at it for five years. We restored the clothes of the expedition members as well as the hundreds of textile fragments found across the campsite. The clothes arrived at the conservation studio in boxes. We unpacked large lumps of balled up, rigid cloth. The bundles were completely covered in polar bear hairs. We knew, of course, that these were the clothes they had died in, and there was something unsettling about knowing that there might be skin or tissue left inside when we started unravelling the stiff fabric, layer by layer. But I'm not very squeamish. It was the week before Christmas. I was working alone downstairs. This particular day I had a pile of mittens to wash, iron and mend. I lined up several buckets of tepid soap water on a table. I put one mitten in each bucket. They were left to soak for a while before I washed them, ever so carefully, just squeezing them a bit, really. It was easy work; I didn't need to pay a lot of attention. But suddenly I noticed that the water in one of the buckets looked odd. It had gone a rusty brown colour. Is that clay? I wondered and took a closer look. That's when I realised the colour was spreading sort of through the wool, from inside the mitten. It was a knitted right-hand mitten. It had belonged to Andrée. And something about this mitten was dyeing the water a rusty brown colour. *Is there something inside?* Without stopping to think, I stuck my hand in there to have a feel. It wasn't until I pulled my hand back out that I heard myself screaming. I was holding three long, grey fingernails."

Today the nails are stored in a box at the museum. I rattle them in my hand. I am holding a small part of Andrée. I can still detect a few thick red stains on the outside of the largest nail. Is it blood? This sample, the only known tissue sample from the expedition, has not shed any light on the cause of their deaths. Researchers analysed the nails twice in the 1990s, using two different methods. They were looking for increased levels of toxic substances and both times they found signs of lead and copper, but the results were inconclusive because there were too many sources of potential error. The nails were not washed before the analysis. The metal is just as likely to have come from the outside of the nail, the result of contact with the cartridges and lead shot Andrée kept in his pocket.

Andrée's hands were not found on White Island, but he must have been wearing the mitten when he died. During decomposition, when his body was being broken down, the nails came loose from his fingers and snagged in the wool. Later, sometime between 1897 and 1930, an animal must have pulled the mitten, and consequently the nails stuck to the inside of it, off his hand. Andrée was wearing mittens when he died. At least on his right hand.

EVENING HAS FALLEN before I finally kill the engine, letting my rental car come to rest. My thighs are numb; I have been driving for so long. Deep in the Finnish forest, among the blueberry bushes and patches of snow that refuse to melt, even though it is the middle of May, lies Nanoq, an arctic museum. I have been told there is a femur here, which was possibly found at the campsite on White Island. The lower halves of Andrée's and Strindberg's skeletons – their femurs, tibias and fibulas – were entire when they were discovered in 1930. But Fraenkel's left femur was never found. It was not mentioned in the autopsy report. Might it have been frozen into the ice at the campsite in 1930, only to thaw out eventually? Could there be a whole femur for us to test for lethal levels of morphine, opium, lead or copper, maybe even cyanide or arsenic? I notice myself thinking us, but really it is just me.

A replica of the first polar church on Greenland has been built on the museum grounds. The bone is stored in its own little glass-top coffin. I open it and place the bone on the altar. It is obvious straight away: damn it, it is from a right leg. But you never know; the autopsy in the basement of Kysthospitalet was rushed and right and left are easily confused. I measure the bone. Check my lists. Measure again, both maximum and bicondylar length. Do the maths.

The bone in my hand is 16 inches long. That means the person to whom the femur belonged was 5 foot 2 inches, +/- 1.2 inches.

5 foot 2 inches. The autopsy report states that Andrée's and Strindberg's femurs were 21 inches. They were, in other words, 6 feet tall. Fraenkel's bones were not measured during the autopsy, but I have no recollection of the expedition consisting of two men of normal height and one very short man. One very short man who also had two right legs.

Stature = 2.38 x femur + 24.18 inches +/- 1.2 inches

BACK AT THE ANDRÉE MUSEUM ONCE MORE. Leaning over, I cup my hands to the glass of the display case in an attempt to make out details in the dark. In the furthest corner of the case, behind union flags and tin cans chewed by polar bears, sits the expedition's medicine box. It measures 16 x 6 x 8 inches. The lid is missing. The box is full of cylindrical wooden tubes, lined up side by side. Many of the tubes look undamaged, despite having been buried under snow and ice for 33 years. The medicine box was found near the tent on White Island. As I stand there squinting, I have an idea. If I examine what the tubes contain, I should be able to deduce which medicines Andrée, Strindberg and Frænkel actually took during the expedition. Andrée very meticulously noted down the symptoms they experienced and the medicines they used in his diaries, but he probably did not bother mentioning things he found too trivial. If I can figure out which medicines they actually used, I will be able to establish what symptoms they really experienced. And if I were to discover previously unknown symptoms, they could affirm or rule out diagnoses potentially associated with a cause of death.

I can also determine which medicines were left untouched. If they did not take a certain type of medicine it would indicate they had no use for it. And if I could tease out what symptoms they did *not* have, I may be able to exclude one or several diagnoses by means of their associated symptoms.

I need help to carry the box to a well-lit backroom. Each wooden tube contains a smaller glass vial, sealed with a cork stopper. I pull up the first vial. The head pharmacist at Stockholm's Lejonet pharmacy labelled each with thorough instructions regarding use and dosage in a spindly hand. Different vials for different illnesses. There are medicines for everything from whitlow, i.e. an abscess of the finger (glass vial 22) and fainting (28) to fever (10 and 12) and aches (5).

THE MEMBERS OF THE EXPEDITION used medicines for the following symptoms: diarrhoea, stomach pains, muscle aches, joint pain, snow blindness, frostbite, abscesses, headaches and acid reflux or gastritis. Some of the medicines are completely untouched: mustard plasters used externally as a warming poultice to dilate blood vessels in cases of frostbite. Capsules to alleviate tonsillitis. None of the analgesics in the medicine box have been used. So they did not have fevers.

Almost all the tubes were still in the medicine box when it was discovered on White Island. All but three. This is important: Andrée, Strindberg and Frænkel had reason to remove three types of medicine from the box during the few days they survived on White Island.

1. Atropine, for use in the eyes to alleviate snow blindness. The tube was found at the campsite.

2. Lanolin, a balm used on frostbitten hands and lips. It was found in Andrée's clothing.

3. Morphine. They had taken the morphine out of the box. The diaries from their march reveal that they used morphine tablets for pain relief when their stomach pains became unbearable. Thus: one or several of them were in pain on White Island before they died. In enough pain to need morphine to ease it.

I try calling

Nils Strindberg's number.

The line at 2090 is engaged.

I AM HOLDING THE PARCEL. I had thought it would be heavier. It is a grey Thursday in June and I am here at my local post office holding what might be Frænkel's rib in my hand. The bone has been sent to me in Stockholm by post. I have just collected it. I stood in line. Imagine if Frænkel had known, as they sailed away from Danes Island in their wool coats and elk skin gloves, calling out *Long live old Sweden!*, that one day his rib would be shoved in a small padded envelope on a shelf at my local post office, between book packages and rustling bags of mail order clothes.

No one knew about this bone. It was stolen from the campsite on White Island. It has been kept secret since 1930. Peter Wessel Zapffe was the photographer on Stubbendorff's expedition. He helped in the excavation of the camp, when the remains were put in boxes for the journey to Tromsø. No one noticed Zapffe sneaking one of the ribs into his bag. He kept the bone at his home for almost 80 years. When Zapffe died, his belongings were donated to the Polar Museum in Tromsø, but instead of being exhibited, the bone was placed in the museum's archive, to which only staff have access. And there it has remained, until now. The rib could belong to any of the members of the expedition, but was most likely, according to the autopsy report, Frænkel's. Good god, a rib! Suddenly there may be a real pathology specimen, which could reveal the cause of death.

THE CEILING OF THE VERTEBRATE ROOM at the Museum of Natural History in Stockholm must be at least thirty feet high. Animal craniums mounted on wooden panels line the walls. Skeletons jostle for floor space. Eighty-six per cent of the world's animal species are represented in the collection. Giant armadillos. Rhinoceroses. Extinct antelopes with twisted horns. Before I start running tests on Frænkel's rib I have to rule out the possibility of it being an animal bone. Sofia Prata, archaeologist and osteologist, is going to help me. On the work bench before us are five large bags of thick, transparent plastic. They contain the complete, unmounted skeletons of every mammal ever found on White Island: polar bear, bearded seal and ringed seal. I have ordered the bag containing the arctic fox as well, even though its ribs are much too small to be confused with those of a human. The ribs of a walrus are too large, but I want to make absolutely sure and not make any assumptions.

We open the plastic bags and pull out the long, dry reference bones from the White Island fauna. We place all twenty-four ribs from each species in order of size on the work surface. Then I open the little envelope.

The bone is bubble wrapped. In addition to the rib bone there is a letter from 2008, in which a professor of forensic medicine in Tromsø affirms that the bone is human. It informs me that it is the second rib from the top, on the left side. The professor sexed the rib as well: *a sturdy man.* I turn the bone over. I am both focused and dizzy at once. I try not to shake. Grey, jagged grains of sand from White Island's beach are wedged into the bone's every imperfection. It is covered in something that looks like moss. Is it residual tissue? I gently poke at the greenish grey threads to see how they are attached. It is just half a bone, roughly 6 inches long, with a round, yellowed head where it was doubly attached to the transverse processes of the vertebra. The other end of the bone has been broken off cleanly. We systematically compare

Frænkel's bone with all the animal bones. When I look up, Sofia Prata's face is serious in the sharp light. There's something about the articular facet, she says. I don't recognise it.

The bone from Tromsø does not quite look like a human bone. The size is just right, but the shape is off. The morphology is identical to that of a polar bear, but it is much too small. The polar bear reference bone on the bench in front of us is more than twice as large. And it cannot be from a polar bear cub, Sofia says; the ossifying growth regions of their skeletons make them easily identifiable.

I put the rib back in the envelope. How could the people in Tromsø have attested to this being a human bone? How could they have been so sure? What do they know that we do not?

What the hell kind of bone is this?

IN ORDER TO EXTRACT ENOUGH DNA to perform species identification, the Swedish National Board of Forensic Medicine requires a tissue sample at least 1.2 inches long. From such a sample they can extract mitochondrial DNA, cross-reference it, and, thus, confirm whether the rib came from an animal or a human with 100 per cent certainty.

In the autopsy room at Stockholm's Department of Forensic Medicine, they help me cut off a small part of the rib. I hold the bone as firmly as I can, as the pathologist starts the whining bone saw. Suddenly it occurs to me that maybe we ought to be wearing respirators rather than surgical masks, in case the members of the expedition did, in fact, die of botulism. The bacterium clostridium botulinum type E can survive in its endosporic form, without any nutrition, in a completely hostile environment, for decades, maybe centuries, only to revive and reproduce when it comes into contact with a more favourable environment (such as the airways or skin of a human). Clostridium botulinum toxin type E is the world's most potent neurotoxin. 150 nanograms is enough to kill if inhaled. 4000 grams would be enough to eradicate humanity.

Wearing significantly more effective respirators, we resume the cutting. I try not to breathe in at all, just out. I do not want to feel lethal paralysis slowly spreading from my face and arms. At least I would have solved the mystery of the cause of death pretty quickly, but I am not sure it is the optimal way of uncovering the truth.

I have a special test tube to post the small bone sample in, but it would drive me insane if the only useable tissue sample from the expedition was lost by some apathetic summer temp worker at the post office. I drive the more than 100 miles down to the National Board of Forensic Medicine in Linköping, with the test tube on the seat next to me. It takes the forensic genetics department two weeks to determine whether the bone really belonged to Frænkel. It does look like a polar bear bone. Just an unusually small one. Is there some other species on

White Island, one I have missed? An animal that looks like a polar bear but is the size of a human. The abominable snowman?

I want it to be Frænkel's rib so badly. Surely the big secret Peter Wessel Zapffe had kept since 1930 cannot be a polar bear rib?

The National Board of Forensic Medicine
Department of forensic genetics and forensic toxicology

Forensic genetic identification

Sample
Bone sample submitted by Bea Uusma

Query
To what species does the bone belong?

Method
The species of the sample has been identified through DNA analysis using PCR technique followed by DNA sequencing. Resulting DNA sequences have been compared with a reference database containing DNA sequences of humans and Scandinavian mammals. The method is not accredited.

Assessment
Tests have established that the DNA sequences found in the sample are identical to the reference sequences of bear (brown bear/polar bear).

Gunilla Holmlund   Andreas Tillmar
Research assistant   Technical molecular biologist

Grenna Museum Polar Centre, Att: Bea Uusma/H Joriksson
Post box 104, 563 22 GRÄNNA

Postal address/visiting address   Phone number   Fax
The National Board of Forensic Medicine   013-25 21 00 switchboard   013-25 21 99
Department of forensic genetics and forensic toxicology 013-31 58 70 forensic genetics
Artillerigatan 12   013-25 21 50 forensic toxicology   Email
587 58 Linköping   reli@rmv.se
Sweden

STRINDBERG'S JACKET IS MADE of thick, dark blue wool. It is of a hunting model fashionable in 1897 and has a number of slanted pockets scattered across the front. Sitting in its display case at the museum, it looks practically new. Having read the conservation report from 1978, I understand why. The textile conservators at the Royal Armoury put 181 man-hours into restoring it. The tattered rags were fitted back together and mended. Where the cloth was beyond repair, parts were cut off and replaced with brand new cloth of the same material, dyed to match the original impeccably. The report tells me what the jacket looked like before restoration: *The flap is missing from the top pocket on the left side. The left front panel is torn, particularly around the armhole. A big slash down the back. The left sleeve is in tatters. The left point of the collar is missing entirely. The lining is very ragged and dirty. Large sections are missing.*

So Strindberg's jacket was torn, ripped to shreds, when it was found on White Island in 1930. Almost all the garments found in the camp were in tatters and covered in coarse white polar bear hair. But there is an important difference: Andrée's and Frænkel's clothes lay strewn about the camp for thirty years, exposed to the ravages of polar bears. Strindberg's jacket was found rolled up next to his sledge. He was buried without a jacket, with three jumpers layered under his blue wool vest, but it is much too cold to go without a proper jacket on White Island in October. Strindberg had not brought another jacket on the expedition. He *must* have been wearing the blue jacket for as long as he was still alive.

The man, or men, who survived Strindberg removed his jacket. They rolled it up, securing the bundle with a belt. And so the jacket lay by a sledge, rolled up, protected from predators, for 33 years. The damage, which the textile conservator needed 181 hours to repair, must therefore have been done before Strindberg died.

I FIND SOME PHOTOGRAPHS from the restoration in a red binder in the Royal Armoury's archive in Tumba. When I compare the pictures taken of the jacket before and after the restoration, I notice that the left front panel had a wide, roughly six inch long cut across the shoulder. The flap of the breast pocket had been ripped off. The cut ran diagonally across the left shoulder and down the sleeve. The damage to the jacket was not confined to the outer layer of wool; it also penetrated the inter-lining and the striped inner lining. There was another cut on the right front panel, where the cloth was torn on the grain at a 90 degree angle.

The blue wool vest in which Strindberg was buried was also mended: *The upper section of the left front panel – from the topmost button hole – is missing entirely. So is the upper section of the left back panel.* During the restoration, the left back and front panels were replaced with new fabric. The photos show a long gash along the side seam of the left back panel, extending from the shoulder all the way down to the waist.

Strindberg's clothes were torn at the left shoulder. The slashes cut through several layers of thick fabric. I read the autopsy report again: *When Strindberg's long johns were rinsed, a pendant with three charms was found: a heart, a cross and an anchor.*

Why did he keep a pendant in his underwear? Had he worn it around his neck, on a chain that had broken? Was there a connection with the tearing? It seems strange that Strindberg would have walked around with charms in his underwear for any extended period of time. It seems likelier that it came loose at the time of his death, and slid down his body. He must have died standing up?

le darling!

It   a long time now since I have spoken
with you. Indeed, since then the situation has
the evening   ca   a large lead we decided to
rearrange our equipment the next day so that
each could haul his own sledge. The method
we have hitherto employed of all three hauling
one sledge and then returning for the ~~others~~
other sledges was too time consuming. On
the 26th July we crossed the lead and on the
other side we unloaded our stores and began
to unpack with a view to leaving some of our
provisions and equipment behind.

10.

Tangents.

I have scaled the treacherous cliffs of the Seven Islands, the northernmost group of islands in all of Svalbard, to look for the remains of the expedition's provisions depots. In a place where no wood exists, a thousand miles north of the tree line, I found one small, sawed piece of wood, a few inches long, with a nail in it. That was it.

I HAVE GONE FOR A FLOOR-LENGTH SKIRT? I never wear long skirts. Furthermore, I seem to have wrapped my scarf around my shoulders as though it were an old fashioned shawl. As though I am trying to dress appropriately, so as not to appear alarmingly hyper-modern to the late-nineteenth century people I suppose I might be about to meet. I am standing in the basement of a block of flats in the Stockholm suburb of Bredäng. Down the stairs to the left, she said, but all I can see here is the door to the basement storage unit and a grey door leading to some sort of bike storage. I really do not believe in this sort of thing. I believe in facts and science. Maybe this was not such a good idea after all.

Just as I turn to leave, the door to the bike storage opens. The psychic looks anything but supernatural. She looks like a regular soccer mum in jeans and a black cardigan. She studies me intently. Then she lets me in. It *is* a bike storage room, with two chairs set out on either side of a small table.

The psychic motions to one of the chairs. I sit down across from her. She shuffles the cards of her tarot deck, then asks me to cut it and place the cards in a large star shape on the table. I venture:

"This might sound weird, but I would like to ask about an old polar expedition that disappeared at the end of the nineteenth cen—"

"ONE AT A TIME!"

The psychic has raised her voice, shouts at the empty room. She sounds stern. I figure she must have heard me wrong:

"So, I'm basically trying to find out what happened to—"

"I SAID ONE AT A TIME!"

This time she looks straight at me. No, she actually looks straight through me. Then she turns around, looking this way and that in the empty room. She sighs.

"There are so many people here to talk to you. Let's go one at a time."

"Is Nils Strindberg here," I ask.

The psychic nods. I'm thinking that since I've come all this way I should just accept whatever comes, even though I am scientifically trained. Otherwise I might as well leave.

"Can I ask him a question?"

She nods again.

"What killed you?"

I just about have time to think that that is not a question one often asks people, before the psychic suddenly closes her eyes. Her head falls forward on her chest. When she starts speaking, her voice is strangely thick. *We finally made it to shore. We are in the tent. I am cold. We were not prepared for this at all.* She falls silent and shudders.

"Yes? And then what happened?" I ask.

She looks up. She is shaking from head to toe.

"I'm sorry," she says, "I have to stop here. I'm too cold."

"No, please, tell me a bit more!"

"No, I'm sorry, I can't catch a cold right now, I'm cooking at the pre-school all of next week. Or wait, he's saying something else. *There is a letter that no one has found. You have to find the letter.*"

What letter? The only letter I know of that no one has read is the one Strindberg dropped from the balloon, but that would be impossible to find. Impossible and unnecessary. Probably dangerous as well. And I do not believe in psychics anyway.

OUR BLACK RUBBER DINGHY pitches in the rough sea as we set our course toward the island. We dodge past ice floes. I have managed to persuade 13 people from my tour group to come with me on this little outing. Fifteen people on the ship raised their hands this morning, but two changed their minds as soon as they spotted the island from afar. *It doesn't even look like an island. It's just a precipice with a cloud on top,* they shouted and shut the deckhouse door against the wind. This is my third visit to Danes Island, the site of the balloon's take-off. This time I have managed to talk the other travellers on the ship into taking a small detour, 12 miles north. Sander Solnes is one of them. He works for the Sysselman, the most senior Norwegian representative on Svalbard, and is responsible for all freeze-dried historical artefacts littering the beaches. Fox traps. Old boots. Relics of hunting and whaling.

All that morning, Sander and I pored over maps and books in the ship's canteen, trying to formulate a plan for our search. Our best clue is one single sentence in Strindberg's almanac. On the 11th July 1897, a few hours after take-off, he wrote: *The tube with my farewell note to Anna was dropped over Vogelsang.* Apart from this statement we have only a handful of sources to work with. Unfortunately, I can hardly claim that the scientific credibility of the material is indisputable.

It consists of:
1. a modern topographic map of the island;
2. a map from *Andrée's Story: The Complete Record of His Polar Flight, 1897*, in which a black line traces the Eagle's route;
and most importantly
3. a sketch of the island, drawn by an eyewitness on the beach of Danes Island in 1897. Someone has added the Eagle into the picture, where it was last sighted, passing over Vogelsang.

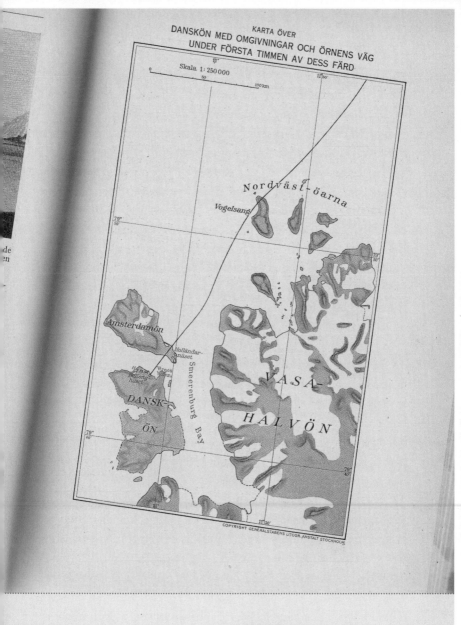

KARTA ÖVER
DANSKÖN MED OMGIVNINGAR OCH ÖRNENS VÄG
UNDER FÖRSTA TIMMEN AV DESS FÄRD

Skala 1: 250 000

Nordväst-öarna

Vogelsang

Amsterdamön

Holländar-näset

Smeerenburg Bay

DANSK-ÖN

VASA-HALVÖN

COPYRIGHT GENERALSTABENS LITOGR. ANSTALT STOCKHOLM

Amsterdamön

Vogelsang

Holländarnäset

At point 1 the Eagle is located directly above Vogelsang.

At points 2 and 3 the Eagle has passed Vogelsang. We think.

VOGELSANG IS LONG AND NARROW, no more than two and a half miles wide. Its highest point is 1,270 feet. Somewhere on this island, wedged between the grey rocks, lies the case with the letter. It was tied with a silk ribbon. It has lain on the island through snowstorms and freezing rain since 1897. Anna did not even learn of its existence until 33 years later. Sander, who is an expert on objects exposed to the arctic climate, is convinced that the case, made of brass or copper, has weathered more than one hundred winters intact. According to Strindberg's notes, the balloon was travelling at an altitude of 2,000 feet when it passed the island, but the sketch makes it look as though it cleared the peaks of the island with no more than 150 or so feet to spare. We have agreed that Strindberg most likely dropped the letter on the plateau that runs between the island's two most northerly peaks. One of the peaks is called Øydehovden. The other does not even have a name.

As I disembark the rubber dinghy I can feel water seeping into my boots. The rocks at the water's edge, covered in green algae, are unbelievably slippery. A wall of enormous jagged boulders rises up before me. The two peaks are lost to the eye, veiled in arctic fog. We are going right up to the top. With every step I take on my way to shore, I can feel, clearly, that no one has ever walked here before. This place is shrouded in a very tangible feeling of solitude.

Sander climbs on ahead. The rest of us follow in single file, struggling to place our hands and feet exactly where he did. It is so terrifyingly steep. The higher we climb, the harder the wind batters us. The straps of my backpack lash at my face, but I am too scared to let go of the rock to tie them down. At least every tenth rock I grab wriggles loose and tumbles down the mountainside. The hard, clacking sound of rock on rock. I climb, slowly, methodically. Leg. Leg. Arm. Arm. I am afraid to turn around; I refuse to look up or down; I just stare fixedly at the next boulder I can hold on to. But out of the corner of my eye, I see billions of crevices, just large enough to hide a cylindrical brass or copper case.

What if Strindberg dropped the letter onto this slope? No. He *must* have let it fall where he thought it could be found.

As soon as I reach the plateau, terror washes over me. I want to climb back down immediately, this feels too unsafe. I am not made for this. I inhale. Yes, I am. And now the worst is behind me, now we are actually on level ground. Now we are inside the cloud we saw from the ship. We have to shout to make ourselves heard over the roar of the wind. We have to stick close together; even up here, in this strange, hazy dream, the polar bear threat is real. I spot the remains of an almost entirely consumed reindeer under a big boulder. Torn patches of white fur litter the mossy ground.

We form a human chain, shoulder-by-shoulder, thirteen wide. Then we start searching the plateau. Sander's GPS has a tracking function and as we trudge back and forth across the plateau we can see a line forming on the display, helping us to avoid covering the same ground twice. We search silently. The only sound is Sander infrequently hollering: *arm's length, arm's length!* to remind us to keep the correct distance from each other. Every time I look into a crevice, I am poised to shout a triumphant HEEEERE IT IIIIS! I know what my voice will sound like and sort of mentally test-shout ecstatically.

Two hours later a nagging worry is creeping into my thoughts: why would Strindberg have thrown the letter down on this plateau? Would he not rather have aimed for the beach, so the crew from Danes Island could simply have rowed over and picked it up?

Five hours later I am thinking: this letter had better be damned good, considering how long we have been looking for it.

Eight hours and twenty minutes later I start doubting. But I tell myself this is just like when you buy Lego for your kids and you sit there with

the instructions and one particular piece is missing. You look and look and look and it is always the same feeling; you feel so certain the piece must be missing; they must have forgotten to put it in the box at the Lego factory, and just when you throw in the towel and get up to leave, the piece appears right in front of you on the table. Suddenly it is just there. I am hoping it will be the same with this tube, as the letter is now, most unromantically, referred to. Suddenly it will just be there, on the ground, right in front of us.

Nine and a half hours later we have covered the entire area. The sea is rough on the way back and when I turn to look at Vogelsang it is completely shrouded in fog. The letter is still out there somewhere. We did not find it.

I'm sitting here turning a small vial of clay over in my hands. The contents are seabed sediment that the researchers on the icebreaker brought back from the North Pole. They lowered a corer to 13,800 feet below the sea ice, and brought up clay from the ocean floor. I unplug the vial. A burnt smell. I can't resist licking it. Immediately regret it as the bitter salt taste spreads through my mouth. What if it's crawling with anaerobic bacteria, of a previously unknown kind? What would I say at the infection unit of the A&E? Pardon, I accidentally ate some clay from the seabed at the North Pole.

11.

The final days.

FOUR DAYS ON WHITE ISLAND, then all writing ceases. Crumbling relics on a barren beach are all that remain of the final days of the expedition. All objects found were brought back. Now there is nothing there but a crag. So far, all research into the expedition has proceeded from the same map. It is a drawing from 1930, showing the location of the bodies and the sledges and the dispersion of the equipment across the campsite. Because there are so few clues, researchers have turned to this map, which is based on a handful of simple sketches, for information. But the map is inaccurate.

In 1998, during an archaeological expedition, topographic measurements of the White Island beach were taken using lasers. When I compare the measurements with the photographs taken on location in 1930, before the camp was excavated, a very different picture emerges. I have to make a new map.

The White Island Camp.

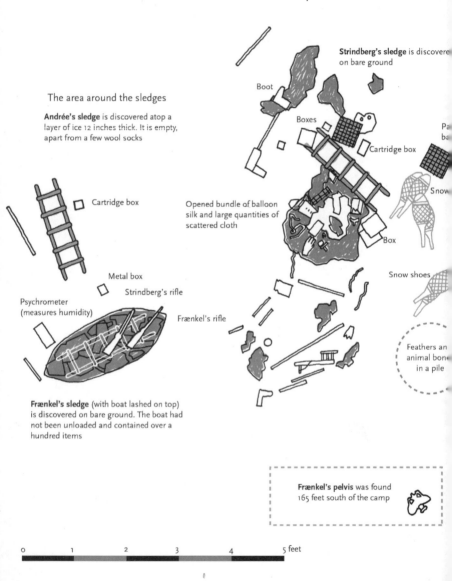

Strindberg's sledge is discovered on bare ground

Boot

The area around the sledges

Andrée's sledge is discovered atop a layer of ice 12 inches thick. It is empty, apart from a few wool socks

Boxes

Cartridge box

Pa
ba

Cartridge box

Snow

Opened bundle of balloon silk and large quantities of scattered cloth

Box

Metal box

Snow shoes

Strindberg's rifle

Psychrometer (measures humidity)

Frænkel's rifle

Feathers an
animal bon
in a pile

Frænkel's sledge (with boat lashed on top) is discovered on bare ground. The boat had not been unloaded and contained over a hundred items

Frænkel's pelvis was found 165 feet south of the camp

0   1   2   3   4   5 feet

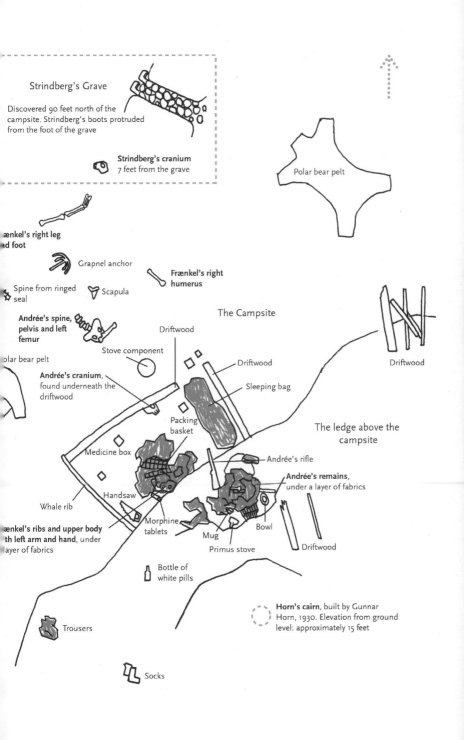

Strindberg's Grave

Discovered 90 feet north of the campsite. Strindberg's boots protruded from the foot of the grave

Strindberg's cranium
7 feet from the grave

Polar bear pelt

ænkel's right leg
d foot

Grapnel anchor

**Frænkel's right
humerus**

Spine from ringed
seal

Scapula

**Andrée's spine,
pelvis and left
femur**

The Campsite

olar bear pelt

Driftwood

Stove component

Driftwood

Driftwood

Andrée's cranium,
found underneath the
driftwood

Sleeping bag

Packing
basket

The ledge above the
campsite

Medicine box

Andrée's rifle

Andrée's remains,
under a layer of fabrics

Whale rib

Handsaw

ænkel's ribs and upper body
th left arm and hand, under
ayer of fabrics

Morphine
tablets

Mug

Bowl

Driftwood

Primus stove

Bottle of
white pills

Horn's cairn, built by Gunnar
Horn, 1930. Elevation from ground
level: approximately 15 feet

Trousers

Socks

THE REMAINS OF THE EXPEDITION'S small camp were discovered 500 feet from the water's edge, in the lee of a low crag. The crag is only a few feet tall and offers poor shelter from the wind. Animals have been in and out of the camp over the years, disturbing items and body parts. Scraps of clothing and human bones were found strewn across the sand beneath the crag. The tent was torn when they found it, but had been pitched along the side of the rock. The groundsheet was still frozen to the sand. The tent was 7.5 feet long and 5.5 feet across at the entrance. The members of the expedition had arranged driftwood and whale ribs in a square against the side of the crag, probably to anchor the tent pegs or the tent, to prevent it being blown away. The square was approximately 6.5 feet wide and 10 feet across.

The remains of Knut Frænkel – his cranium, upper body, left arm and hand – were found within the confines of the square, under a broken packing basket. (Parts of his right arm, right leg and foot were found scattered through the camp. His right forearm and left leg were never found.) Frænkel lay perpendicular to the crag wall. His head was frozen to an indentation in the rock. He lay on his left side, his arm bent, his hand under his head. His fingers, to which nails and soft tissue were still attached, were flexed, but witnesses insisted that they had not looked convulsively clenched. He did not have mittens on. Several people who were present when Frænkel was found have, independently of each other, reported that his hair was brown or reddish brown and that he wore a hat. The hat is not mentioned in any subsequent documentation. The packing basket that covered Frænkel's body was shredded, its contents dispersed. The body was covered in several layers of fabric, frozen outer garments and jumpers, among other things. What was left of a woollen blanket was spread across the groundsheet of the tent. The clothes Frænkel had been wearing were torn and scattered, but the buttons were still done up, which must indicate that he was wearing the garments when he died. He wore six layers of clothing on his upper body. A broken bottle of brown glass leaned against the rock next to his face. Its contents are unknown. Next to Frænkel's head, wedged between the crag and the snow, lay a glass vial, labelled *Morph.*, containing morphine tablets. The vial was almost empty. It was stoppered. The exact location of the vial of morphine is only mentioned in the earliest reports. *Frænkel died with morphine to hand.*

Behind Frænkel's body there was a small aluminium box tied to two unopened copper cases laden with tin cans. Three brown notebooks, a pair of sunglasses, a pocket knife and more tin cans were found in the bundle of clothes strewn around the body. The bundle also contained Frænkel's meteorological records (in which the last entry was made on the 3rd October 1897) and one of Strindberg's almanacs (in which the last entry was written, in pencil, on the 7th October). A cooking pot, a fruit knife and a spoon were discovered on a small ledge above Frænkel's head. The expedition's three-man sleeping bag was found empty in a crumpled heap by the edge of the tent. During the excavation of the tent area, a saw, an aluminium plate and a saucepan full of ice, which was later found to contain the remains of what appeared to be lobscouse, were discovered.

Frænkel's long johns and trousers were found, in tatters, some way from the tent. There were no cartridges in the pockets. His right leg, the foot of which had no boot on, was found. His pelvis was discovered 165 feet south of the tent. A pair of broken boots, which must have belonged to Frænkel, were found at the campsite. The leather laces were untied, as though he had taken them off. *Frænkel wore neither boots nor mittens when he died.*

Salomon August Andrée's cranium was found underneath one of the pieces of driftwood used to demarcate the tent area. It lay directly on the ground, under a layer of ice eight inches thick. The cranium wore a hat. Inside the hat, which was frozen to the skull, there was organic material consisting of either fur or human hair. The hat was in tatters and was discarded at the scene. The majority of Andrée's remains were found on a rock shelf, three feet up the side of the crag. At first it was thought that his body was in a sitting position, the upper body reclining against the rock, but when the bundle of cloth from which his bones protruded was examined more closely, it became clear that large parts of the body were missing.

Andrée's lower legs and feet were intact, dressed in long johns, trousers and boots. The legs were stretched out in front of him. The bundle of clothes consisted of both rags and undamaged garments, socks, mittens and a hat. The clothes Andrée had been wearing on his upper body when he died were found shredded on the ledge – a jacket, among other things, covered in polar bear hair, and missing one sleeve. The inner pocket of the jacket contained Andrée's not yet finished second diary, a pencil and a pedometer. The last diary entry had been made on the 8th October. Andrée's spine, pelvis and left femur were found just outside the squared off tent area. His hands were never found, but three nails were discovered inside a mitten during the textile conservation in 1978. *Andrée wore both boots and mittens when he died.*

Andrée's first diary was found underneath the bundle of clothes by his body. It had been wrapped in a jumper packed with senne grass, a sedge used to insulate boots. The whole package was wrapped in balloon cloth. The last note in the diary was made on the 2nd October. A little ways above the bundle on the crag, lay the expedition's Primus stove, still filled with paraffin. When the Primus stove was tested after 33 years on White Island, it worked. The ledge also held an aluminium mug and a bowl containing food residue. Andrée's rifle and an axe lay by his side. The rifle pointed down toward his feet. With the help of photographs from 1930, researchers have concluded that the rifle was probably loaded, because the hammer was half-cocked, but there is no way of knowing for sure. Andrée's trouser pockets contained matches and rifle cartridges. *Andrée was the only member of the expedition who was armed.*

Almost all books about the Andrée expedition state that Andrée and Frænkel passed away peacefully, side by side in the tent. Researchers have assumed that the tent stretched across the part of the crag where Andrée was found. But that cannot be true; the tent was much too small. *Unlike Frænkel, Andrée was not in the tent when he died.*

Outside the squared off tent site the ground was littered with a variety of items, among others, parts of the expedition's cooking apparatus, the medicine box, a polar bear pelt and parts of Frænkel and Andrée's skeletons. On a slope between the crag and the beach an unmarked bottle was discovered, three-quarters full of white tablets, probably sweets. A few feet from the tent, five or six pieces of driftwood were piled against the crag. A bit further away there was another pile of less substantial wood.

Strindberg's empty sledge was discovered roughly 13 feet from the tent. On the ground next to it was a pile of items, which must previously have been packed onto the sledge, which included a bundle of balloon cloth, ripped open to reveal fabric and clothes, two broken packing baskets, a cartridge box and several scientific instruments. This is where Strindberg's letters and photos were found, along with letters that had belonged to Frænkel and one of Frænkel's almanacs. Three pairs of snowshoes lay on the ground next to the sledges. One pair was assumed to be unused, since it was tied together with fine string.

Andrée's and Frænkel's sledges were found roughly 30 feet from the tent. Andrée's sledge was empty, save for a handful of wool socks. The sailcloth boat was lashed on Frænkel's sled. It held hundreds of items. The sack containing Frankel's personal effects, which weighed

37 pounds, had been removed from the boat. Left was an abundance of clothing, such as woollen jumpers, mittens, a shoe, a boot and a leather hat, as well as two of the three rifles brought on the expedition (Strindberg's double rifle and Frænkel's single-shot rifle). *Two of the expedition's three rifles were stored 30 feet away from the tent when the last person on White Island died.*

Nils Strindberg was the only member of the expedition to be given a grave. The man, or men, who survived Strindberg chose to bury him in a narrow crevice between two large rocks, 92 feet from the tent. They must have squeezed the body in to make it fit. The grave was covered with a thick layer of stones, roughly four and six inches across. Strindberg's booted feet were sticking out the foot of the grave when he was found. He was wearing three jumpers and a vest, two pairs of long johns and trousers of blue cloth. Someone had removed Strindberg's jacket before the burial. It was found at the outskirt of the camp, rolled up and secured with a belt. On his feet, Strindberg wore double socks and boots packed with shoe hay. The black and white chequered hat he wore in photographs from their march across the ice was found at the outskirt of the campsite. His cranium, separated from the body, was discovered ten feet from the foot of the grave.

I stare at the map. It has to mean something. I just do not know what.

LENNART KJELLANDER is a forensic technician and crime scene investigator with Sweden's National Bureau of Investigation. Normally, when investigating a case, there is a crime scene for him to visit, where a thorough crime scene investigation can be conducted. Moreover, he normally prefers for as little time as possible to have passed since the event in question occurred. In this case it has been more than a hundred years.

We take my revised map, photographs from the scene and what I have uncovered in records and eyewitness reports as our starting point. We know what was in their pockets. We know the location and position in which their bodies and equipment were found. We know what had been unpacked from the sledges. And what had not been unpacked. The location of many items must be disregarded, since animals have rummaged through the campsite over the years. There were also signs of human activity. A crime scene investigation seeks to identify objects, the relative relationships of which can provide clues regarding cause and effect. Such clues are crucial to the accurate reconstruction of events. We are looking for *significant events*, which can be linked together to form a plausible *chain of events*.

Not every question can be answered by a crime scene investigation. Some facts will remain unknown. It is important not to fill the gaps with speculation, because that undermines the validity and credibility of the entire analysis.

We go through the campsite, detail by detail. A new picture slowly emerges.

[x] Andrée wore mittens, boots and a hat when he died. He was warmly dressed, as though intending to spend time outside the tent.

[x] Andrée was sitting on a rock ledge. He was not inside the tent when he died. He was found with his legs stretched out in front of him. Had a polar bear dragged the body onto the ledge it would have ended up in a very different position. Therefore Andrée must have died sitting on the ledge.

[x] Andrée kept the rifle by his side and seven cartridges in his pocket. Clearly he felt it was important to be able to defend himself.

[x] Andrée had his diary with him on the ledge. It had been wrapped in water resistant material to protect it from damage. It was the only diary in the camp treated with such care. Was it a symbolic act? Did he want to preserve it for posterity? Did Andrée know he was about to die?

[x] Andrée had Strindberg's purse in his pocket. He was looking after Strindberg's things. Therefore he must have been alive when Strindberg died. Neither Frænkel nor Strindberg had effects belonging to the other members of the expedition in their pockets. Why did Andrée, and not Frænkel, keep Strindberg's personal belongings?

[x] Frænkel wore neither boots nor mittens. He could not possibly have traipsed around White Island without boots in October. There was only one place they did not wear boots: in the sleeping bag. Since Frænkel wore neither boots nor mittens it is likely that he died in the sleeping bag.

[x] The morphine had been taken out of the medicine box. During their march, the morphine tube was kept in the box. On White Island it was unpacked. The glass vial of morphine was found next to Frænkel. Was he in need of pain relief?

[x] Frænkel had no rifle to hand. Moreover, he had no ammunition in his pockets. He died unarmed. Was he too weak to defend himself? If Frænkel had survived both Strindberg and Andrée, it is unlikely that he, as the last survivor on White Island, would have crawled into the sleeping bag unarmed. Unless Frænkel and Andrée died simultaneously, Andrée survived Frænkel. The last person to have died ought surely to be the one with a rifle by his side and ammunition in his pocket.

[x] Strindberg's and Frænkel's rifles lay atop the stores in the boat, 30 feet from the tent. What were their rifles doing in the boat? During the march they all carried their own gun. There is something transitory about the placement of the guns, as though they had been put aside, for just a moment.

[x] Strindberg was buried without his jacket. The man, or men, who survived Strindberg and removed his jacket, thought it could be put to better use. It follows that that person did not believe he himself was about to die.

[x] Strindberg's jacket was torn. The jacket was rolled up and secured with a belt. The jacket lay on White Island, protected from scavengers, for 33 years. When it was found, slashes across the left shoulder and sleeve were discovered. These slashes were most likely made while Strindberg was still alive.

[x] Strindberg had a pendant in his long johns. Did the necklace around his neck break and slide down his underwear while he was still upright?

Strindberg died before Andrée.
Frænkel died before or at the same time as Andrée.
Whoever died last did not bury whomever died second. Did he not have enough strength left? Or not enough time?

I HAVE SPENT THE WHOLE AFTERNOON at the museum, reading a collection of letters from Knut Frænkel's brother. One hour left before they close and I have to drive back to Stockholm. I flip through the catalogue of the items brought back from White Island. Each object stored at the museum has its own catalogue card and number. Items 536 and 537 are the double long johns Nils Strindberg was buried in on White Island. The long johns. I had no idea they still existed. I was sure they had been discarded sometime in the 1930s. In the museum's basement there are boxes of material too damaged to restore, but I was given to believe they mostly contained socks and old pieces of string. One hour left before they close.

I request the box. I unwrap the sheets of pink tissue and place the two pairs of long johns side by side on the table. They smell like death. I try to stretch the crumpled, sandy fabric. At first I fail to notice it. I stare at them, my mind blank. It is so difficult to assess what you see, when you do not know what you're looking for. Real evidence does not announce its presence. But then I check myself. Several times now I have let myself believe that I have solved the mystery. I do not want to get worked up again, so when I feel my excitement building, I do my best to stay calm. Nevertheless, my heart is in my mouth. Both pairs of long johns are missing a leg. The fabric of both right legs has been torn, high up on the thigh. I try to smooth down the creased wool to examine the edges, but it is not until I turn the long johns over that it becomes clear. On the back of the long johns Strindberg wore when he died, the ones he was buried in, which have been protected from predators and storms by two feet of rock for 33 years, the fabric has been torn off diagonally. The tear runs from the crotch to the right hip. There are dark stains on the fabric. It actually looks like blood.

Something has torn the legs off the long johns. Could the damage have been done in 1930, when they discovered Strindberg? Maybe the sealers used some sharp implement to prise his body from the crevice? No,

it simply does not add up. Even a quick glance reveals that the fabric was not cut, as would have been the case if the damage had been caused by a sharp tool. The fabric was ripped.

Something has ripped the right leg off both pairs of long johns. When I study the edges more closely I can make out tears: at even intervals, there are unmistakable slashes in the fabric. I count five sharp points where the fabric has been ripped. It looks like claws.

There is no way around it now. I have no choice, I have to go there. To the *inaccessible island.*

12.

An island of ice.

I HAVE ORGANISED MY OWN EXPEDITION. Its only objective is to reach White Island. For six months I have worn myself out trying to get the project financed and find a ship that can take me there. The fact that I have my own expedition is, of course, no guarantee of success. Every day, this whole summer, I have checked met.no at five past one. At 1pm they publish updated ice maps. They are maps drawn from satellite data, where areas of pack ice are assigned one of four different colours, depending on the proportion of the sea's surface that is covered. *Very Close Drift Ice*, when the surface is 90–100 per cent covered, is red on the maps. It changes daily. All it takes is one storm to make what was open water fill with new ice floes from the north in a matter of hours.

Green ice, *Very Open Drift Ice* (up to 40 per cent ice cover), poses no threat to my ship. It can handle shorter distances through *Open Drift Ice* (up to 70 per cent ice coverage). But it is no icebreaker. If we encounter *Close Drift Ice* or *Very Close Drift Ice*, we will have to turn back. My head is aching; for months I have been using the power of my mind to push ice away from White Island. But there is something unusual about this summer. It is unseasonably warm. Last week the ice sheet broke up and since then, the ice around White Island has been green on the map. When we left the pier in Longyearbyen two days ago, it was still green. Now we do not know anymore. We are far from mobile reception and satellite updates.

IT IS 10.57 P.M. I have not seen land for three and a half days. The captain has just informed me that the waters are open the whole way. In two hours and three minutes' time, the life I have lived for the last fifteen years, *before White Island*, will end and another life, *after White Island*, will begin. I lie in bed in my cabin, fully dressed under double duvets and a blanket. I wish I were more excited, but really I just want to be left alone, deep under my covers.

As though I was about to face something very difficult.

An hour and forty-two minutes to go. I am so nervous I think I might throw up. One hour and thirty-nine minutes. I can't stay in bed. I head out on deck, my eyes fixed on the wet decking, anxious not to slip. I walk along the railing, all the way to the prow. Then I look up. The sky and the sea blend in a rich, slate blue colour. But straight ahead, between the sea and the sky, there is a bright white light. I almost have to squint. It lights up the whole horizon.

It is White Island.
White Island is glowing.

ONE STEP FROM THE RUBBER DINGHY to the water's edge. My next step will be my first on White Island. I have studied the old black and white photographs of this beach hundreds of times. I have opened them in Photoshop to sharpen the focus and zoom in, to get inside them, as close as possible. But it is only when I am really here, my boots in the sand, that I understand what it is like. You cannot feel the wind in the pictures. You cannot feel the sting of millions of grains of sand blowing across the shore of White Island on your cheek. And no matter how long you stare at the photographs from 1930 you cannot fathom that the real picture extends beyond the photo's edge. The photo ends at 9 by 12 inches, but in reality the picture continues indefinitely. In one half of my field of vision the Arctic Sea fades into the sky. White Island's glowing glacier fills the other. It is impossible to tell from the black and white photographs, but beyond the brown shore the glacier rises up like a gigantic, white wall. The only thing that is real, when you are right here, is this strip of beach, 10,000 by 1,000 feet. There is nowhere to go from here.

I move slowly toward Andrée's campsite. I know my way around, even though I have never been here. I have walked this way so many times. The beach is lined with small meltwater streams from the glacier. The air is filled with an icy white haze, even though it is quarter to two in the morning and the wind is blasting my face with fine, wet sand that gets in my mouth, my eyelashes, my boots and every crease in my clothes, which in less than an hour have changed colour, darkened by the damp. My Performance Shell Active Pro Gore-Tex trousers feel heavy and cling at the knees and even though I am wearing three layers of underwear I can feel the damp soaking right through. The ground is littered with driftwood, brought to this place from Siberian rivers by the currents. I try lifting one. It is slippery. It is too heavy for me to even shift. I am approaching the camp now and my movements are sluggish, like in a dream, even though I have never been more awake.

I have carried this place inside me for so long, and now that I am here it is as though I am wandering around inside myself.

I am wandering around inside myself now.

I RECOGNISE ANDRÉE'S CRAG, despite approaching it from the wrong direction. It is a lot lower than the photographs make it look. Why did they decide to haul their heavy sledges all the way up to this particular spot? It does not seem logical. There are several other places along the shore that would give better shelter from the wind, deep sand dunes, bigger crags where they could have pitched their tent in a less exposed position. Why did they choose this lousy campsite which does not even offer protection against the wind, I think to myself, and then I suddenly get it. The wind. The wind is blowing straight from the north. The wind is almost always northerly in this part of the Arctic. But this low crag, which they picked to shelter their camp for a whole winter, the spot where I am standing right now, is the only outcrop on the beach that protects against a southerly wind. When Andrée came here, a southerly wind must have been blowing.

It takes my eyes a while to adjust from black and white to colour, but then I suddenly know where I am. I am standing at the exact spot where Fraenkel died. I take two steps up the crag. I sit down exactly where Andrée was sitting when he was found, my legs stretched out like his were, and when I raise my eyes I see exactly what he saw.

I am looking straight at Strindberg's grave.

WHEN ANDRÉE OPENED THE TENT FLAP on the 9th October 1897 it had finally stopped snowing. The shore was bathed in a blue light. It was already late afternoon. They had needed their rest. Now it was time to get to work. Strindberg and Frænkel were lugging pieces of driftwood for the hut when they noticed the polar bear approaching. She must have come down from the glacier. They shouted to scare her off, but she seemed unperturbed. The bear took her time, moved in slowly, eyes fixed on the seal meat. Strindberg dashed over to chase her away.

When Strindberg was no more than a few feet from the polar bear she looked up from the seal meat, shifting her attention. A look of surprise in her eyes. Then she reared up on her hind legs. The first blow knocked him over. A supine prey makes everything so much easier. The polar bear clamped her jaws around Strindberg's head, biting and shaking. Frænkel ran toward the bear, shouted, pelted it with everything he could get his hands on. His rifle was still in the boat, far beyond reach. Andrée had had his rifle slung over his shoulder, but aiming was difficult; he was afraid of hitting Strindberg. The sharp bang of the first shot scared the polar bear; it relinquished Strindberg and lumbered off.

Strindberg left in a crumpled heap in the snow. His clothes black against the whiteness. Andrée kneeled down next to the body. He scanned the surroundings in every direction, but he could not make out which way the bear went. Had she run up the glacier? The visibility was too poor; it was getting darker now.

The sound of straps from their packs flapping in the wind. Frænkel moaning. Was he struck? Come here, lie down in the tent. Andrée got the morphine out and the water bottle. Three tablets. Now swallow. Crawl into the sleeping bag. You're cold.

When dawn came Frænkel's condition had worsened. The moaning had softened into a whimper. Andrée had spent the night on guard duty outside the tent, in case the bear decided to return, but now he went over to Strindberg. Hauling someone with no muscle tone is heavy work. He had to set the body down from time to time, force himself to breathe more slowly. He did not have the strength to drag him very far; the first crevice would have had to do. He reached into Strindberg's pocket. Pulled out his purse, cartridges. Andrée removed his jacket, setting it aside for the coming winter. It was difficult for him to place the first stone on Nils Strindberg's bearded cheek. Then another. And another. His face was hidden under the stones. He was gone. *Our Father who art in heaven.* Stone upon stone. Covering his hand, the one with the ring. *Hallowed be thy name.* Andrée looked around. *Thy kingdom come.* Was the bear coming back?

Frænkel had gone silent in the tent. He was still. And very cold. Andrée took two steps up the crag to the small ledge. Sat down. Only now did he notice the first aurora borealis of the polar night billowing across the sky. In ten more days, the sun would set on 1897. He was sitting in a place that did not exist. He did not even know what the island was called. The polar bear was certain to return. And there was not just one, she had simply been the first. For four months he would have to sit, alone, in complete darkness. The next sunrise would be in February. He would never get off this island. He would never be able to haul his sledge with the boat and the stores to the depot on Spitsbergen on his own, come spring. Every day, for the rest of his life, he would have to be on polar bear duty. One day he would get distracted. He wrote no farewell note. He fetched his diary from the packing basket – the proof that his expedition had not been a complete failure. On the first page, proudly and clearly: ANDRÉES POLAR EXPEDITION. All of this must be worth something. Something. Pulling out a woollen jumper, he wrapped it around the book for protection. He had no need for a woollen jumper now. He wrapped the bundle in balloon cloth, to make it waterproof.

Salomon August Andrée, head engineer at the Royal Patent and Registration Office, days away from his 43rd birthday, sat alone on a rock shelf above a silk tent. He had seen what bears are capable of. The loaded gun on his left. Seven cartridges in his right trouser pocket. Four tablets from the vial of morphine. He did not want to die. Just swallow. He looked straight at Strindberg's grave. He closed his eyes. Opened them again. Strindberg's grave. He closed his eyes.

In this moment you are probably sleeping sweetly and maybe you dream of your Nils. I hope your dreams are happy and beautiful and that you do not torment yourself with anxious thoughts. And then when you wake it will be Sunday and papa will be there and I am certain you will have a lovely day together. Yes, these things occupy my thoughts constantly these days, one has a lot of time to think here and it is so delightful to have such pleasant memories and such happy prospects to think of as I have!

The law of entropy states that all processes in the universe strive toward maximum disorder. The universe is supposed to get messy. The atoms are supposed to intermingle. Living matter is characterised by low entropy, order, and we humans try to structure and organise; we write long lists and count and re-count, but nature always strives toward high entropy with a force infinitely more powerful than ours. Ten thousand-year-old glaciers slide slowly but irrevocably down mountainsides. Glacial water mingles with sea water. My body heat mingles with the cold outside my Gore-Tex jacket. It's 10 degrees below freezing. If I died on this beach it would take my body 30 and a half hours to cool to the ambient temperature.

Nature devours us. Icy winds and rain and salt and snow erode us, decompose us, reduce us to molecules, carbon compounds; the covalent bonds between the carbon and hydrogen atoms break. Our atoms mingle with the brown grains of sand on the only small strip of beach on White Island.

Anna, 4th May 1897.
The picture was found among Nils' belongings

Well, once we had managed to pull the sledge out again we had to pilot ourselves across a few floes separated by leads. This we did by pushing the ice floes so that it they ended up side by side. With the larger floes this was slow work of course. Then we finally reached a large ice field across which we have walked for 1 or 2 miles with our sledges, each loaded with about 350 pounds so they are very heavy and during the last hour we had to resort to all 3 of us pulling one sledge at a time. Now we have made camp next to a picturesque bit of ice and pitched our tent. In the tent we have a sleeping bag in which all three of us now lie side by side. It is a squeeze but we get along famously. Well, I have so much to write to you about, but I must go to sleep now. Goodnight my   rling!

13.
To where
I cannot follow.

NEVER RETURNED

Spain City
By Sha

Thirty-three years ago this dark-eyed young Swedish girl, Anna Charlier, now Mrs. Gilbert Hawtrey, Concord, N. H., said good-bye to her fiance, Nils Strindberg, brilliant young scientist of Stockholm university. He left with the Andree balloon expedition, headed for the North Pole, but never returned and was never heard from again.

ANNA CHARLIER IS BURIED in plot 6640 at the public cemetery in Torquay. She was 78 years old when she died. She shares the grave with her husband, Gilbert Hawtrey. But there is no heart in her body. Her body has no heart.

The 4 September 1949 would have been Nils Strindberg's seventy-seventh birthday. His brothers had gathered on Stockholm's Northern Cemetery. They were old men by then, in coats, hats. It was early morning. Chilly. Unbeknownst to outsiders, they were secretly carrying out Anna Charlier's final wish. After she died, her heart was cut out of her body and cremated. And without applying for the appropriate permits, without involving anyone, they were opening Nils Strindberg's grave to lower a small silver chest into it.

The chest held Anna Charlier's heart.

My son often asks me: what does it matter what they died from? They died on White Island. They're dead. It was more than a hundred years ago.

There will never be an answer. The more I learn about the Andrée expedition, the more unsure I feel about what really happened. Can we really be sure they actually died? Were the bodies discovered on White Island really theirs? The image fades. At length it becomes completely white.

Maybe I was looking for something else.

I hate being cold. I'm wildly uninterested in putting myself through ordeals. Definitely no adventurer. And yet I've spent half of my adult life trying to become a part of the expedition, more than a hundred years too late. Sometimes I think I became a doctor just to be able to find out what happened. I thought I could follow them, but I never get close enough. I thought this would pass when I finally made it to White Island. I was wrong. We have taken the same arctic photographs, theirs in black and white, shot with a fifteen pound box camera, mine with my smartphone. I have collected colour samples from the ice. Andrée has collected bits of clay in parcels.

Three men, who spend every day battling across the pack ice to reach a place where the ground can hold their weight, but who remain forever in the same place as the ice beneath their feet drifts in the opposite direction. A love story, with a very sad ending. I know exactly what that's like. We belong together. The expedition and I.

A FAREWELL CARD FROM ANNA CHARLIER is pasted to the first page of Nils Strindberg's almanac. A hand-drawn picture of a balloon that has just left the ground. Were he to have looked really closely he would have seen that Anna has pencilled herself into the picture, on the ground beneath the balloon. Long skirt, her hair in a bun. Waving her handkerchief.

And if he had looked even more closely he would have seen that she has drawn three men aboard the balloon. One of them is raising his hand to wave back.

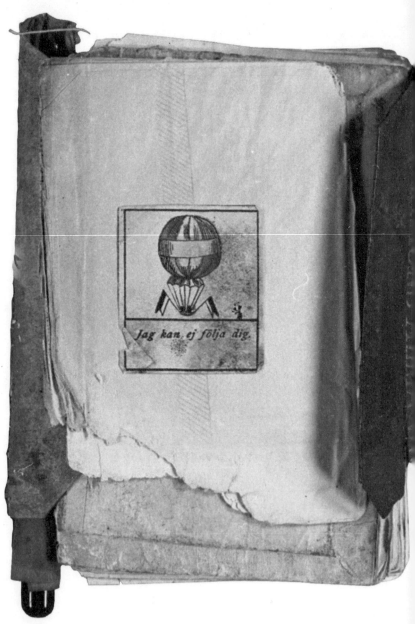

Jag kan, ej följa dig.

To where I cannot follow.

CAUSES OF DEATH.

CARBON
MONOXIDE
POISONING

OXYGEN
DEPLETION
IN THE TENT

ALGAE SOUP
POISONING

SCURVY

TRICHINOSIS

VITAMIN A
POISONING

BOTULISM

HYPOTHERMIA

LEAD
POISONING

GUNSHOT
WOUND

POLAR BEAR
ATTACK

MORPHINE

Carbon monoxide poisoning caused
by the Primus stove

Strindberg was dead. The blizzard howled outside. As the tent on White Island was gradually snowed under, the ventilation worsened. Frænkel and Andrée used the Primus stove to cook inside the tent. Did they slip into a stupor, poisoned by carbon monoxide gas, rendering them unable to get out?

Carbon monoxide gas is a by-product of the combustion of organic compounds, such as the fuel of a Primus stove. The person breathing it will notice nothing at first, because the gas is colourless and odourless. In high concentrations it is also lethal. The first symptoms of poisoning are headaches, light-headedness and fatigue. This is followed by confusion, nausea, vomiting and loss of consciousness. In high doses carbon monoxide impedes the body's ability to metabolise oxygen, which, in turn, leads to death by asphyxiation.

There are a number of known cases of carbon monoxide poisoning in the history of polar exploration, among others the four members of the Stefansson expedition, who died in their sleep in a tent on Wrangel's Island in 1914.

OXYGEN
DEPLETION
IN THE TENT

ALGAE SOUP
POISONING

SCURVY

TRICHINOSIS

VITAMIN A
POISONING

BOTULISM

HYPOTHERMIA

LEAD
POISONING

GUNSHOT
WOUND

POLAR BEAR
ATTACK

MORPHINE

OXYGEN
DEPLETION
IN THE TENT

ALGAE SOUP
POISONING

SCURVY

TRICHINOSIS

VITAMIN A
POISONING

BOTULISM

HYPOTHERMIA

LEAD
POISONING

GUNSHOT
WOUND

POLAR BEAR
ATTACK

MORPHINE

Reasons to believe carbon monoxide poisoning caused their deaths	Reasons to believe carbon monoxide poisoning did not cause their deaths
It is an acute condition, which could have killed three people in the course of a few hours	The Primus stove still contained 1.3 pints of paraffin when discovered in 1930. If they had died with the stove still lit, all the paraffin should have been consumed
	The Primus stove was not in the tent when they died: it was found on Andrée's ledge, nearly three feet above the tent
	Even allowing for the fact that polar bears would have rummaged through the camp, it is unlikely that bears would have taken the Primus stove out of the tent to place it on the ledge

Can be rejected

Suffocation caused by oxygen depletion in the tent

Did they get snowed in during the blizzard and suffocate inside the tent?

In cases of gradual oxygen deprivation, the body reacts to the hypoxia with heart palpitations, headaches, shortness of breath, impairment of judgement and tunnel vision. But only a deeply sedated person could sleep through acute oxygen deficiency. A healthy person would wake in a panic and attempt to get outside for air.

Reasons to believe oxygen deprivation caused their deaths	Reasons to believe oxygen deprivation did not cause their deaths
An acute condition, which could have killed three people in the course of a few hours	The same reasons that pertained to carbon monoxide: Andrée did not die in the tent
	Oxygen deprivation caused by a lack of oxygen would wake a sleeping person
Can be rejected	

CARBON MONOXIDE POISONING

OXYGEN DEPLETION IN THE TENT

ALGAE SOUP POISONING

SCURVY

TRICHINOSIS

VITAMIN A POISONING

BOTULISM

HYPOTHERMIA

LEAD POISONING

GUNSHOT WOUND

POLAR BEAR ATTACK

MORPHINE

Algae soup poisoning

Strindberg made a soup from algae found in the ice. They did not see the connection themselves, but after eating the soup they developed severe digestive problems. Could the food poisoning have been lethal?

They mention making algae soup twice in the diaries, on the 21st and 23rd of August. They also ate something they termed plash algae, a concoction of algae and water. According to the diaries they ate plash algae at least six times.

There are no known cases of this kind of poisoning in the history of polar exploration.

Reasons to believe algae poisoning caused their deaths	Reasons to believe algae poisoning did not cause their deaths
The algae clearly contained something that did not agree with their digestive systems. The first time they ate algae soup they had diarrhoea for 4 days afterwards	They should have succumbed sooner, not more than a month after eating the soup for the first time
Can be rejected	

Scurvy

The body's reserves of vitamin C last for three months. The march across the ice took three months. No fruit, no vegetables. Just some algae in a soup no one liked. Did they die of scurvy after reaching White Island?

When the body's stores of vitamin C are depleted, the formation of new connective tissue is impaired. This leads to bleeding under the skin, particularly on the legs, and bleeding gums and mucous membranes. Other symptoms include depression, weakness, pain and paralysis of the legs, followed by open, suppurating wounds and tooth loss. Left untreated, scurvy eventually leads to death.

Scurvy was one of the most common causes of death among early polar explorers and arctic whalers. At the end of the nineteenth century, 26 per cent of all Norwegian whalers wintering on Svalbard suffered from scurvy. Nine per cent died as a result.

Reasons to believe scurvy caused their deaths	Reasons to believe scurvy did not cause their deaths
Some symptoms that may be indicative of scurvy seem to fit: Frænkel experienced leg pains. Both Frænkel and Strindberg had suppurating abscesses. The diaries mention their extreme fatigue	The symptoms that could be indicative of scurvy arose too early in the march
	There are no mentions of skeletal changes or tooth loss in the autopsy report
	Their food contained raw meat as well as blood, both excellent sources of vitamin C

Can be rejected

CARBON MONOXIDE POISONING

OXYGEN DEPLETION IN THE TENT

ALGAE SOUP POISONING

SCURVY

TRICHINOSIS

VITAMIN A POISONING

BOTULISM

HYPOTHERMIA

LEAD POISONING

GUNSHOT WOUND

POLAR BEAR ATTACK

MORPHINE

Trichinosis contracted from polar bear meat

Did Andrée, Strindberg and Frænkel die of the same illness, having consumed large quantities of trichinella infested polar bear meat?

Trichinella is a parasite that lives in meat. Trichinella larval worms survive freezing but die when heated above 67°C. In the 1950s, a Danish doctor called Tryde had a small sample of polar bear meat found at the campsite analysed. Two of five samples were found to contain trichinella larval capsules. Tryde's theory, to which he dedicated a whole book, suggests that Strindberg died of congestive heart failure caused by the trichinosis. Frænkel and Andrée succumbed soon after, side by side in the tent, fatally weakened by trichinosis.

Trichina infected meat contains encapsulated larvae. When the meat is consumed, the capsules dissolve in the stomach. A female larva can produce several thousand larvae, which spread to the muscles, where they eventually become encapsulated. The first symptoms occur some weeks after consumption of infected meat and include temporary diarrhoea and stomach pains. This phase is easily confused with regular stomach flu. The parenteral phase, the main symptoms of which are high fever (in 88 per cent of cases), swelling around the eyes, muscle pain and diarrhoea, begins 18–20 days after meat consumption. Patients almost always present with headaches. In some very rare cases the condition can be fatal as a result of unusual complications caused by cardiomyopathy, pneumonia or blood clots. The mortality rate is 0.2 per cent.

New research reveals that as many as 50 per cent of the polar bears on Svalbard may be infected with trichinella. Several trichinosis epidemics were reported on Greenland in the 1940s and 50s, with 420 confirmed cases. Since the 1950s, only isolated cases of trichinosis in humans have been reported.

Reasons to believe trichinosis caused their deaths	Reasons to believe trichinosis did not cause their deaths
They consumed large quantities of (often raw) polar bear meat, at times as much as 3.7 lbs. per person per day. Since they probably ate trichinella infested meat on several occasions, they may have suffered a massive infection	Given that the mortality rate of trichinosis is very low, it is unlikely that all three men would have succumbed to it simultaneously
Some of the symptoms of trichinosis (diarrhoea, stomach pains, muscle pains and headache) fit what we know about the state of the members of the expedition	None of the members of the expedition had used the analgesic medications contained in the medicine box. Fever is not mentioned anywhere in the diaries. Fever is one of the most common symptoms of trichinosis
Trichinella infected meat was, indisputably, found at the campsite	

There may have been underlying trichinella infections,
but they would not have been fatal

CARBON MONOXIDE POISONING

OXYGEN DEPLETION IN THE TENT

ALGAE SOUP POISONING

SCURVY

TRICHINOSIS

VITAMIN A POISONING

BOTULISM

HYPOTHERMIA

LEAD POISONING

GUNSHOT WOUND

POLAR BEAR ATTACK

MORPHINE

Vitamin A poisoning from seal liver

During the last three weeks of their march across the ice, they ate parts of a bearded seal. Their consumption included seal liver, which is poisonous. Did they die of hypervitaminosis A?

Mammals store vitamin A in the liver. Vitamin A is toxic in anything but minimal quantities. In high doses it can even be lethal. Boiling and freezing is not enough to break down vitamin A. Andrée, Strindberg and Frænkel were aware of the toxicity of polar bear liver and avoided eating it, despite the food shortage. They did, however, over the course of three weeks, eat the liver of a seal they shot, since they did not know that seal liver also contains high levels of vitamin A (12,000–14,000 IU/g, compared to polar bear liver: 15,000–30,000 IU/g).

Acute hypervitaminosis A occurs after consumption of a dose of 1–1.5 IU. In order to consume such a quantity, the members of the expedition would have had to eat 3–4 ounces of bearded seal liver per person. Initial symptoms include nausea and vomiting, severe headaches, light-headedness, irritability, extreme fatigue, blurred vision and light sensitivity. In some cases there are stomach pains and diarrhoea. Symptoms arise 4–8 hours after consumption. Several days later the skin of the hands, face and feet will peel off. In rare cases the poisoning is fatal.

A few cases of vitamin A poisoning in the Polar Regions have been recorded, when expeditions have consumed large quantities of liver due to starvation or ignorance. Merz and Mawson both fell ill during their expedition to Antarctica 1911–1914 after eating their sled dogs, livers and all, due to food shortages. Merz is believed to have died of acute hypervitaminosis A.

Reasons to believe vitamin A poisoning caused their deaths	Reasons to believe vitamin A poisoning did not cause their deaths
They ate the liver of a bearded seal during their final weeks on the ice. 3–4 ounces is a small portion considering that a bearded seal weighs in between 440 and 550 pounds with a liver said to weigh 40 pounds	They shot the bearded seal on the 19th September. The diaries make no mention of illness in the days that followed
	The mortality rate is low
Skeletal parts from a seal were found at the campsite on White Island	It is improbable that Andrée and Frænkel would have been capable of burying Strindberg while themselves dying from hypervitaminosis A
Andrée, Strindberg and Frænkel's vitamin A levels were presumably elevated after repeatedly consuming bearded seal liver. They also ate blubber from a ringed seal, which is another source of vitamin A, if not quite as plentiful	

It is not unthinkable that the condition could have led to an inability to keep warm, resulting in fatal hypothermia

CARBON MONOXIDE POISONING

OXYGEN DEPLETION IN THE TENT

ALGAE SOUP POISONING

SCURVY

TRICHINOSIS

VITAMIN A POISONING

BOTULISM

HYPOTHERMIA

LEAD POISONING

GUNSHOT WOUND

POLAR BEAR ATTACK

MORPHINE

CARBON
MONOXIDE
POISONING

OXYGEN
DEPLETION
IN THE TENT

ALGAE SOUP
POISONING

SCURVY

TRICHINOSIS

VITAMIN A
POISONING

BOTULISM

HYPOTHERMIA

LEAD
POISONING

GUNSHOT
WOUND

POLAR BEAR
ATTACK

MORPHINE

Botulism from seal or tinned fish

Were they paralysed by the extremely toxic bacterium clostridium botulinum type E, ingested with seal intestines, which are known to contain such bacteria? Or were they poisoned by the tinned fish in their stores?

Clostridium botulinum toxin type E is one of the world's most potent toxins. It is produced by the bacterium clostridium botulinum, which inhabits the seabed sediment of the Arctic Ocean, and ends up in the stomachs and intestines of seals, since they feed near the ocean floor. The toxin can also be produced in tinned foods, particularly tinned fish that has not been sufficiently heated before preservation. The toxin is heat sensitive; boiling destroys it. The bacteria survive freezing, but growth is inhibited in temperatures below +3°C.

Botulism is a rare condition, but several arctic cases have been recorded, caused by the consumption of aged seal meat or seal intestines. Botulism from seal and botulism from tinned fish lead to the same type of paralysis, which proceeds bilaterally from the cranial nerves. Initial symptoms include light-headedness, fatigue, dilated pupils, double vision, droopy eyelids, sore throat, dry mouth and speech difficulties. The descending paralysis affects all voluntary muscles in the body. Death occurs when the respiratory muscles become affected.

Reasons to believe botulism caused their deaths	Reasons to believe botulism did not cause their deaths
Acute poisoning would have progressed rapidly, causing the more or less simultaneous deaths of all three members of the expedition	It is improbable that Andrée and Frænkel would have been capable of burying Strindberg and piling rocks on his grave if they were themselves dying of botulism
Botulism from seal: The last seals – two ringed seals and a bearded seal – were shot on the 19th September. The bearded seal provided enormous quantities of food. It took a long time to finish, which may have given the bacteria time to grow. The bearded seal was shot on the 19th September and is mentioned in the diaries on the 29th September. At that point the meat was already ten days old. Bones from the bearded seal were found at the campsite on White Island	The position of Frænkel's body, his arm bent and his hand balled, is not consistent with the paralysis associated with botulism Botulism from seal: For the bacteria to grow, a temperature of at least +3° is required. After the 19th September (when the last seal was shot) the temperature never rose past -0.5°. Hence, it was too cold
Botulism from tinned fish: They brought tinned fish on the expedition, at least nine tins and cans of sardines. Two empty sardine cans were found on White Island	

Botulism from seal meat: can be rejected
Botulism from tinned goods: rare, but not definitely implausible

CARBON MONOXIDE POISONING

OXYGEN DEPLETION IN THE TENT

ALGAE SOUP POISONING

SCURVY

TRICHINOSIS

VITAMIN A POISONING

BOTULISM

HYPOTHERMIA

LEAD POISONING

GUNSHOT WOUND

POLAR BEAR ATTACK

MORPHINE

Hypothermia

Snowstorm on White Island. Hypothermia, dehydration and exhaustion caused the worn out members of the expedition to slip into an apathetic state. Did they increasingly struggle to keep warm and eventually freeze to death?

The theory posits that the cold alone did not kill the members of the Andrée expedition, but rather a combination of cold, dehydration and exhaustion. Being cold is dehydrating: blood vessels contract, causing a rise in blood pressure, which in turn leads to increased urinary output. Physical activity and diarrhoea also lead to dehydration. On modern, physically draining polar expeditions, a fluid intake of 7–9 pints per day is necessary to prevent dehydration. For a person suffering from fluid deficiency, maintaining a sufficiently high body temperature is challenging. When core body temperature drops below 34–33°C, paradoxical undressing may occur (caused by a sudden feeling of warmth), but this is more commonly associated with rapid drops in temperature. A body temperature below 33°C causes lethargy and eventual loss of consciousness. Below 28°C there is a risk of fatal tachycardia.

Hypothermia is one of the most common causes of death among polar explorers, often in combination with scurvy. But surviving a winter in the Polar Regions is not uncommon. Nansen and Johansen, for example, spent 8 winter months side by side in a hollow on Franz Josef Land in 1895–96.

Reasons to believe hypothermia caused their deaths	Reasons to believe hypothermia did not cause their deaths
Recurring diarrhoea during the march across the ice led to chronic dehydration (Frænkel was worst affected)	Were they really dehydrated? They melted snow for drinking water every time they cooked, using a device connected to the Primus stove. Their meals also contained fluids. The diary mentions soups, gruel (Mellin's food) mixed with meltwater, hot chocolate, bouillon, cordial, plash algae (algae and water), coffee and polar bear and seal blood
Constant physical exertion during the march caused increased sweat production, which in turn leads to dehydration	
For several months, damp clothes, wet socks and less than waterproof boots had made staying warm virtually impossible After reaching White Island, they were cooped up in the tent. Inactivity leads to decreased heat production	They do not seem to have suffered from diarrhoea on White Island. The last time diarrhoea is mentioned in the diaries is more than a month before they reach land
Frænkel and Strindberg's foot injuries during the march may have been caused by frostbite	They write nothing about frostbite. Many of the clothes in their packs, such as mittens, boots and socks, were never used. Strindberg's clothes and shoes were not used after his death. Andrée and Frænkel did not die side by side in the tent, in an attempt to keep each other warm
	Only three mentions of feeling cold are recorded during the 87 days of their march. The last temperature report, on the 3rd

CARBON MONOXIDE POISONING

OXYGEN DEPLETION IN THE TENT

ALGAE SOUP POISONING

SCURVY

TRICHINOSIS

VITAMIN A POISONING

BOTULISM

HYPOTHERMIA

LEAD POISONING

GUNSHOT WOUND

POLAR BEAR ATTACK

MORPHINE

CARBON
MONOXIDE
POISONING

OXYGEN
DEPLETION
IN THE TENT

ALGAE SOUP
POISONING

SCURVY

TRICHINOSIS

VITAMIN A
POISONING

BOTULISM

HYPOTHERMIA

LEAD
POISONING

GUNSHOT
WOUND

POLAR BEAR
ATTACK

MORPHINE

October, reads -6.2°C. (As compared to Nansen and Johansen, who survived five months of temperatures as low as -44°C)

Were they really exhausted? The subject of the final diary entry is their dissatisfaction with storm-induced house arrest; they want to go outside: ... to move about a little...

Andrée and Frænkel may ultimately have died of hypothermia, but it is unlikely to have been the primary cause of their death

Lead poisoning from the tin cans

At the end of the nineteenth century tin cans were often sealed with lead solder. Were they poisoned by the tin cans? Were they gradually poisoned every time they ate tinned food?

The symptoms of chronic lead poisoning are subtle. The initial signs are lack of initiative and fatigue. Additional consumption results in stomach cramps, lack of appetite, constipation or diarrhoea, weight loss, muscle and joint pain and blue gums. Continued consumption leads to abdominal colic: severe, acute stomach pain and impaired coordination, confusion, memory loss and paralysis. Spasms and loss of consciousness eventually lead to death.

Lead poisoning has been the death of many a polar explorer. The most common victims were those whose diet was restricted to tinned goods, brought in tins sealed with lead. Seventeen wintering seamen died of lead poisoning at the Swedish research station on Spitsbergen in 1872–1873. The crew of the Franklin expedition were poisoned in the middle of the nineteenth century. Their tin cans were sealed with lead solder. All the crockery on their ship was lead-glazed. The insides of the drinking water pipes on board their ship were lead-coated. Furthermore, their tobacco, biscuits and chocolate were all wrapped in lead-covered tin foil.

CARBON MONOXIDE POISONING

OXYGEN DEPLETION IN THE TENT

ALGAE SOUP POISONING

SCURVY

TRICHINOSIS

VITAMIN A POISONING

BOTULISM

HYPOTHERMIA

LEAD POISONING

GUNSHOT WOUND

POLAR BEAR ATTACK

MORPHINE

CARBON
MONOXIDE
POISONING

OXYGEN
DEPLETION
IN THE TENT

ALGAE SOUP
POISONING

SCURVY

TRICHINOSIS

VITAMIN A
POISONING

BOTULISM

HYPOTHERMIA

LEAD
POISONING

GUNSHOT
WOUND

POLAR BEAR
ATTACK

MORPHINE

Reasons to believe lead poisoning caused their deaths	Reasons to believe lead poisoning did not cause their deaths
The tin cans in the expedition's stores were sealed with lead solder	Correlative symptoms were not present: no signs of mental sluggishness or lack of initiative
Two separate analyses of Andrée's nails have detected high levels of lead	The results of the nail analyses are difficult to assess; there are many potential sources of error. The presence of lead in the nail could have been caused by contact with the lead cartridges and shot Andrée had in his pocket
Some of the symptoms experienced by the members of the expedition are consistent with lead poisoning: fatigue, stomach and joint pain	
Frænkel's deteriorating mental state during the march could be a sign of lead poisoning	Their rate of consumption ought not to have caused a fatal accumulation of lead

Improbable, as their exposure to lead was too insignificant

Gunshot wound

Did the psychological strain on White Island lead to a fatal shooting? As the result of conflict or as an act of mercy? Or was someone shot by accident?

Depending on how you read them, the diaries could be hinting at an underlying schism between Andrée on the one hand and Strindberg and Frænkel on the other. Did Strindberg and Frænkel get along better and pair up, on account of both the age difference between them and Andrée and the fact that the whole shambolic expedition had been his idea? Andrée wrote in his diary that Strindberg and Frænkel would sit there, freezing, while he reconnoitred, and that Strindberg and Frænkel were homesick, unlike him. Frænkel had to haul a much heavier sledge than the others throughout the march. Both Strindberg and Frænkel injured their feet, while Andrée got on better. On the 20th September, Andrée wrote in his diary that disagreements had been surfacing: ... while we have not been able to avoid the beginnings of open discord. Nevertheless I hope that this seed will not take root and grow.

Reasons to believe gunshot wounds caused their deaths	Reasons to believe gunshot wounds did not cause their deaths
Strindberg's death is not mentioned in the diaries	There were no gunshot injuries on craniums or bones
The subtext of Andrée's diary can be seen to hint at a conflict between Andrée on the one hand and Strindberg and Frænkel on the other	Lack of motive – the strength of three people would be needed to make it back to civilisation
Accidental shooting: possibly Strindberg. Murder: unlikely	

CARBON MONOXIDE POISONING

OXYGEN DEPLETION IN THE TENT

ALGAE SOUP POISONING

SCURVY

TRICHINOSIS

VITAMIN A POISONING

BOTULISM

HYPOTHERMIA

LEAD POISONING

GUNSHOT WOUND

POLAR BEAR ATTACK

MORPHINE

Polar bear attack

Did a polar bear catch Strindberg unawares on White Island? During the march, they appear to have been oblivious to the threat polar bears posed. Were Andrée and Frænkel killed by polar bears as well?

Modern arctic expeditions use dogs, trip wires attached to firecrackers around their tents, starting pistols (warning shots) inside their tents and rifles in the outer tents to protect against polar bears.

A polar bear's diet consists mainly of seal, primarily blubber. The meat is only of secondary interest. If she is very hungry she may break bones to get at the marrow. In rare cases, polar bears have even been known to eat skeletal parts. Polar bears have no fixed territory; they roam the sea ice, up to 60 miles a day, looking for food. A polar bear can smell a seal from 18 miles away. When a polar bear has killed its prey she immediately drags it a way off before eating. It is not unusual for her to return to the same kill several times.

When the ice melts in the Arctic during summer, polar bears follow the edge of the ice north, since that is where the bearded seal makes its home. Bears who have been trapped on the land in autumn have very limited access to prey and will consequently modify their behaviour, becoming more aggressive in their search for food. A hungry polar bear will eventually eat anything.

The area around Svalbard has always crawled with polar bears. Many attacks on humans are documented in the annals of polar exploration. Johansen narrowly escaped being killed by a polar bear on his trek across the pack ice with Nansen in 1895. The 80 attacks on humans that occurred on Svalbard 1971–1995 left 10 people injured, four of whom died of their injuries. All attacks happened without warning. None of the people injured or killed were armed. In three of four cases the attack began with the polar bear rearing up and striking with a front paw, followed by biting in the head and neck region. Injuries have included fractured skulls, mandibles, faces and necks as well as loss of skin and soft tissue on head, neck, arms and legs.

Reasons to believe a polar bear attack caused their deaths	Reasons to believe a polar bear attack did not cause their deaths
The members of the expedition demonstrated an utter lack of respect for polar bears on several occasions during the march across the ice. On the 17th September, for instance, Strindberg rushed a polar bear trying to poach their seal. Andrée mentions spotting polar bears on White Island twice, including the day before all entries cease	Polar bears on White Island ought to have been more interested in the meat store than in the members of the expedition
One or several of them seem to have required morphine while on the island	If Strindberg was killed by a polar bear, Frænkel could be expected to have fetched his rifle from the boat and kept it to hand
The expedition's meat store and cooking attracted hungry polar bears. Polar bears on White Island would have had poor access to seals, since bears should normally have moved further north by October	Andrée's position, sitting on a rock shelf, his legs parallel and his rifle by his side, suggests that he sat down by his own volition. It does not suggest a polar bear dragged his body there. If Andrée was killed by a polar bear, the polar bear would most likely have dragged the body away
Strindberg died before the others (at least before one of the others) Strindberg's charms were found in his underwear – did a blow to the neck cause the chain to break? Strindberg's jacket showed signs of damage likely to be indicative of the way he perished. The right legs of Strindberg's double pair of long johns were torn off	The attacking pattern of polar bears is inconsistent with the fact that Frænkel remained by the tent, where he must have lain prior to passing away

Strindberg likely, Frænkel possibly, Andrée less likely

- CARBON MONOXIDE POISONING
- OXYGEN DEPLETION IN THE TENT
- ALGAE SOUP POISONING
- SCURVY
- TRICHINOSIS
- VITAMIN A POISONING
- BOTULISM
- HYPOTHERMIA
- LEAD POISONING
- GUNSHOT WOUND
- POLAR BEAR ATTACK
- MORPHINE

CARBON
MONOXIDE
POISONING

OXYGEN
DEPLETION
IN THE TENT

ALGAE SOUP
POISONING

SCURVY

TRICHINOSIS

VITAMIN A
POISONING

BOTULISM

HYPOTHERMIA

LEAD
POISONING

GUNSHOT
WOUND

POLAR BEAR
ATTACK

Morphine

Did Strindberg take his own life on White Island? Or did Frænkel and Andrée kill themselves following Strindberg's death, when they realised what lay ahead? Struggling to survive a winter in a tent in one of the most polar bear-rich areas of the Arctic. Maybe the last survivor had no wish to go on and, so, killed himself by overdosing on drugs?

The isolation and peril a wintering in the Polar Regions entails inevitably takes its toll on a person's mental state. Symptoms of winter-over syndrome include insomnia, cognitive impairment, depression, anxiety and irritability, as well as tension and conflicts within groups. Research shows that expedition leaders, who by virtue of their position bear a greater burden of responsibility, experience more anxiety than other participants.

Two of Andrée's medicines could be used for suicide through overdose: morphine and opium. The morphine pills had been taken out of the medicine box on White Island. There were at most 28 morphine pills left in the vial when they reached the island. Less than 4.5 ounces of morphine, the equivalent of 12–20 pills, is a lethal dose, but smaller doses can induce deep unconsciousness, which can in turn result in fatal hypothermia. (The opium pills were, with a morphine content of no more than 10 per cent, less potent. A deadly dose could not have been achieved with opium alone. The opium had not been taken out of the medicine box on White Island.)

The history of polar exploration abounds in stories of winter-over syndrome. In some cases whole expeditions, such as the Belgian expedition to Antarctica in 1898, have suffered from depression. During the Greely expedition, which sought to establish a scientific research station on Ellesmere Island in 1881–1884, the isolation and psychological stress led to suicide and cannibalism. Only 6 of the 25 members of the expedition survived.

Reasons to believe morphine caused their deaths	Reasons to believe morphine did not cause their deaths
Theirs was a hopeless situation	Suicide was seen as unacceptable at the time
The morphine had been unpacked on White Island ll	
	Apart from the note about Frænkel on the 9th August, the diaries make no mention of depression or despair among the members of the expedition
Andrée's project had failed utterly and one (or possibly two) members of the expedition had perished	
Andrée wrote in his diary during the balloon journey: We feel we could easily face death now that we have done what we have done Andrée had previously suffered depression-like symptoms, during the wintering at the Swedish Research Station on Spitsbergen in 1882–1883	There was still morphine and opium left in the glass vials. If the intention was suicide the vials would, perhaps, more likely have been completely emptied
	Strindberg had a very good reason to fight to make it back, since he was recently engaged
During their march across the ice, Frænkel was the most psychologically affected. On the 9th August, for example, Andrée wrote that *little appears to remain of his moral strength*	

Strindberg unlikely, Frænkel possibly, Andrée possibly

CARBON MONOXIDE POISONING

OXYGEN DEPLETION IN THE TENT

ALGAE SOUP POISONING

SCURVY

TRICHINOSIS

VITAMIN A POISONING

BOTULISM

HYPOTHERMIA

LEAD POISONING

GUNSHOT WOUND

POLAR BEAR ATTACK

MORPHINE

Sources

FACTS REVIEWED BY
Anders Larsson, Head Librarian, Gothenburg University Library, Gothenburg

FACTS RELATING TO CAUSES OF DEATH REVIEWED BY
Mark Personne, Medical Consultant, Director, The Swedish Poisons Information Centre, Stockholm

SOURCES
PRIMARY SOURCES
- Andrée's main diary(Record no APXP 458 C)
- Andrée's secondary diary (Record no APXP 520)
- Strindberg's main log book (Record no APXP 6)
- Strindberg's secondary log book (Record no APXP 266)
- Strindberg's almanac from 1896 (Record no APXP 268)
- Strindberg's almanac from 1897 (Record no APXP 462)
- Strindberg's almanac from 1897 (Record no APXP 460 C)
- Strindberg's annotation almanac from 1897 (Record no APXP 459 A and B)
- Frænkel's meteorological journal (Record no APXP 460 A)
- Facsimiles of the Andrée Expedition diaries, The Centre for History of Science, The Royal Swedish Academy of Science
- The Grenna Museum Archive
- The Nils Strindberg collection, The Manuscript Collection, the National Library of Sweden
- Salomon August Andrée, surviving documents, The Manuscript Collection, the National Library of Sweden
- Packing lists from the 1896 Andrée Expedition. In private ownership
- Anna and Occa receive a telegram: Occa describing Anna's reaction and his own feelings in a letter to Sven Strindberg, Nils' brother. 22 July 1897. In private ownership

REPORTS
- Broadbent N., Olofsson J. *Archaeological investigations of the S.A. Andrée site, White Island, Svalbard 1998 and 2000.* Umeå University, Department of Archaeology and Sami Studies, 1998 and 2000.
- *The Swedish–Norwegian commission for the conservation and examination of the Andrée materials.* Copy of case no 34/1930 B, Tromsø Magistrates' Court. Grenna Museum.
- *The Swedish–Norwegian commission for the conservation and investigation of the Andrée materials. Copy of case no 35/1930 B, Tromsø Magistrates' Court.* Grenna Museum
- Hedrén G. *Record of the post-mortem examination of the remains of the members of the S A Andrée North Pole Expedition 2-4 and 16-18 September 1930.* Grenna Museum
- Lithberg N. *A record of the repatriated remains of the S A Andrée Polar Expedition 1897, brought back from the White Island aboard m/s Bratvåg and preserved in Tromsø, 2-8 September 1930.* Grenna Museum. This protocol exists in two versions, one handwritten, the other typed. They are not completely identical

- Stubbendorff K. *Receipt for the m/s Isbjörn discoveries*. Tromsø, 16 September 1930. Grenna Museum
- Törnvall G. *Documents from White Island. An examination of the history and future of the material*. University of Gothenburg, Department of Environmental Sciences and Conservation. MA dissertation, 2002
- *Textile conservation report*. The Royal Armoury, Skokloster Castle, The Hallwyl Museum, 1978
- Uusma Schyffert B. *Causes of Death of the Andrée Expedition*. Karolinska Institutet, 2010

SCIENTIFIC ARTICLES

HYPERVITAMINOSIS A

- Carrington-Smith D. "Mawson and Mertz: a re-evaluation of their ill-fated mapping journey during the 1911–1914 Australasian Antarctic expedition", *The Medical Journal of Australia*, 2005
- Hathock J.N., Hattan D.G., Jenkins M.Y., McDonald J.T., Sundaresan P.R., Wilkening V.L. "Evaluation of vitamin A toxicity", *American Journal of Clinical Nutrition*, 1990
- Käkelä R., Hyvärinen H., Käkelä A. "Vitamins A1 (Retinol) A2 (3,4-Didehydroretinol) and E (alphatocopherol) in the Liver and Blubber of Lacustrine and Marine ringed seals (Poca Hispida sp)", *Comparative Biochemistry and Physiology part B: Biochemistry and Molecular Biology*, 1997
- Lewis R.W. "The vitamin A content of polar bear liver: Range and variability", *Comparative Biochemistry and Physiology*, 1967
- Penniston K.L., Tanumihardjo S.A. "The acute and toxic effects of vitamin A", *American Journal of Clinical Nutrition*, 2006
- Rodahl K., Moore T. "The Vitamin A content and toxicity of Bear and Seal liver", *Biochemical Journal*, 1943

LEAD POISONING

- Aasebo U., Kjaer K.G. "Lead poisoning as possible cause of deaths at the Swedish House at Kapp Thordsen, Spitzbergen, winter 1872-3", *British Medical Journal*, 2009
- Kowal W., Krahn P., Beattie O. "Lead levels in human tissues from the Franklin Forensic Project", *International Journal of Environmental Analytical Chemistry*, 1989
- McCord C.P. "Lead and lead poisoning in early America", *Industrial Medicine & Surgery*, 1953

BOTULISM

- Personne M. "Andréeexpeditionens män dog troligen av botulism", *Läkartidningen*, 2000
- Hauschild A.W.H., Gauvreau L. "Food-borne botulism in Canada (1971–1984)", *Canadian Medical Association Journal*, 1985
- Horowitz B.Z. "Polar poisons: did botulism doom the Franklin expedition?", *Journal of Toxicology – Clinical Toxicology*, 2003
- Sobel J. "Botulism", *Clinical Infectious Diseases*, 2005
- Smith G.R., Turner A., Till D. "Factors affecting the toxicity of rotting carcasses containing Clostridium botulinum type E", *Epidemiology and Infection*, 1988
- Sörensen H.C. "Botulism in Ammassalik", *Ugeskrift for laeger*, 1993

POLAR BEAR ATTACK

- Risholt T. "Man and polar bear in Svalbard: a solvable ecological conflict?", *International Journal of Circumpolar Health*, 1998

MORPHINE
– Steine K., Röseth A.G., Sandbaek G., Murrison R., Slagsvold C.E., Keller A. et al. "Økt kortisolnivå, frostskador og påvirkning av muskler og skelett under ekstreme polarforhold", *Tidsskrift for den norske lægeforen*, 2003
– Steine S., Steine K., Sandbaek G., Röseth A.G. "En polarexpedition i motbør – opplevelser og psykiske reaksjoner", *Tidsskrift for den norske lægeforen*, 2003
– Palinkas L.A., Suedfeld P. "Psychological effects of polar expeditions", *Lancet*, 2008

COLD
– Oumeish Y.O., Parish L.C. "Marching in the Army: Common Cutaneous Disorders of the Feet", *Clinics in Dermatology*, 2002
– Granberg P.O. "Cold Physiology and Cold injury", *Proceedings of the Fifth International Conference of Environmental Ergonomics*. Maastricht, Nederländerna, 1992

SCURVY
– Baron J.H. "Sailor's scurvy before and after James Lind – a reassessment", *Nutrition Reviews*, 2009

TRICHINOSIS
– Darwin Murrell K., Pozio E. "Worldwide Occurrence and Impact of Human Trichinellosis, 1986–2009", *Emerging Infectious Diseases*, 2011
– Hill D.E., Forbes L., Zarlenga D.S., Urban J.F. Jr, Gajadhar A.A., Gamble H.R. "Survival of North American genotypes of Trichinella in frozen pork". *Journal of Food Protection*, 2009
– Kocicka W. "Trichinellosis: human disease, diagnosis and treatment", *Veterinary Parasitology*, 2000
– Møller L.N., Petersen E., Kapel C.M., Melbye M., Koch A. "Outbreak of trichinellosis associated with consumption of game meat in West Greenland", *Veterinary Parasitology*, 2005
– Nelson G.S. "More than a Hundred Years of Parasitic Zoonoses: with Special Reference to Trichinosis and Hydatid Disease", *Journal of Comparative Pathology*, 1988
– Schellenberg R.S., Tan B.J., Irvine J.D., Stockdale D.R., Gajadhar A.A., Serhir B. et al. "An outbreak of trichinellosis due to consumption of bear meat infected with trichinella nativa, in northern Saskatchewan communities", *Journal of Infectious Diseases*, 2003
– Larsen T., Kjos-Hanssen B. "Trichinella sp. in polar bears from Svalbard, in relation to hide length and age", *Polar Research*, 1983

Photographs and Images

PHOTOGRAPHS
Nils Strindberg / Grenna Museum, The Andrée Expedition Polar Centre
Front endpaper, 17, 56–57, 64–65, 245
Unknown photographer / Grenna Museum, The Andrée Expedition Polar Centre 21, 31, 36, 69, 96, 97, 176
Unknown photographer / The Nils Strindberg collection at the National Library of Sweden, with the kind permission of Henrik and Staffan Strindberg 73
Sigge Eriksson 85
Henrik Schyffert 15, 89
Hilda Hahne 231
Simon Rudholm 212–213
Johan Sandström 195
Hofphotograph Hahn Nachf Dresden, with the kind permission of Birgitta Bååth 27
The Centre for History of Science, the Royal Swedish Academy of Sciences 39, 183
Gunilla Törnvall / The Centre for History of Science, the Royal Swedish Academy of Sciences 107, 252
Bea Uusma 1, 51, 81, 83, 203, 217, 233, 247
Sander Solnes 163, Back endpaper

IMAGES
Bea Uusma 169, 171, 173, 175, 220–221
Kari Modén Title Pages, Table of Contents, 23, 47, 53, 80, 87, 104, 188
The National Board of Forensic Medicine 198
Nevada State Journal 248
Med Örnen mot polen 209
Ingen fruktan, intet hopp 209

Acknowledgements

Grenna Museum.

A big, warm thank you to Lotta and Emi.

Martina, dearest, without you this book would be nothing but scattered sentences on random scraps of paper.

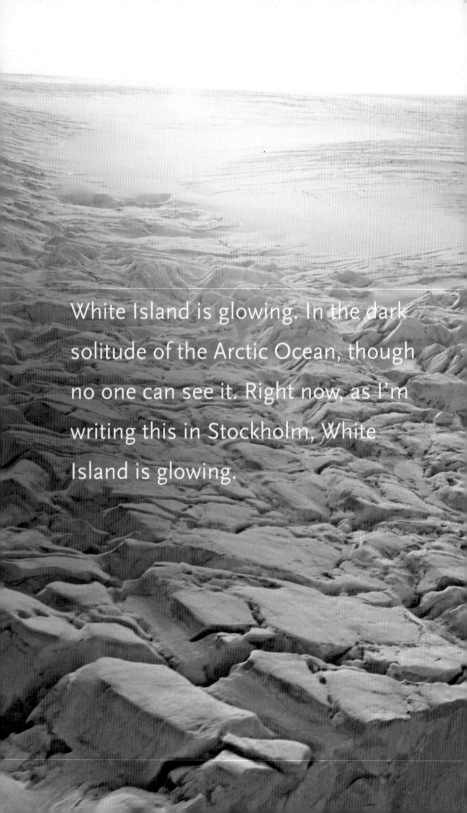

White Island is glowing. In the dark solitude of the Arctic Ocean, though no one can see it. Right now, as I'm writing this in Stockholm, White Island is glowing.